The BUSY BODY

in

The Basque Country,

France and Sicily

Mary Jane Wilson

Waldo Bruce Publishers, Inc., Dallas, Texas

ISBN: 978-0-9963298-0-4
Cover Design: Stefan Merour (Photo by Susan Carpenter)
Illustrations: Courtesy of Carnegie Library of Pittsburgh
and Sanctuaire de Notre-Dame de La Salette, La Salette, France
Photographs: Marty Ledenham, Julie Wilson and Brian Wilson

Travel with the Busy Body through France and Sicily

IN PARIS WANDER through churches and parks, and take a boat ride under the Bastille. Outside Paris, visit the American Cemetery, once the site of a hermitage where Thomas Jefferson often retreated. Visit Alexandre Dumas' Château de Monte Cristo. His motto carved above the stairway says, "I love those who love me." Practically every actress in France loved him—and proved it.

Tour castles and museums. At the château in Amboise on the Loire River where Leonardo da Vinci stayed, a tour ends with a display of forty intricate machines built by da Vinci and duplicated by IBM. Visit the castle in Angers built by King St. Louis IX, then continue to Rochemenier near Samur, where people lived in caves until 1930.

In the Vendée region near Cholet, attend a spectacular outdoor evening extravaganza, *Le Puy du Fou*, commemorating the history of the Vendéans from the Middle Ages. Cannons roar, and a blazing château by a lake burns before your eyes with a riotous display of fireworks in the dark sky.

At La Rochelle in the Maritime Museum, a multimedia film celebrates generations of fishermen who risked their lives fishing for cod in Iceland, 1400 miles away. You will never forget the roar of water crashing on the deck and men with ice-covered beards battling fierce waves.

From Angoulême, cruise along the Charente River with a stop to sample cognac, and take a spectacular boat ride from La Malene through a canyon on the River Tarn.

Mary Jane with the Foreign Legion in Marseille

Get acquainted with the Busy Body's famous dead people, like French King Louis XI, the "Spider King" who trapped people in a web of intrigue: "I am like a woman. When anyone tells me anything in an obscure manner, I must know at once what it is all about." Except on State occasions, he was one of the worst-dressed kings in history—he wore either a riding outfit or drab pilgrim garb. But whatever he wore, his clothes smelled wonderful—like crushed violets. Violets became the perfume of French kings.

Meet seventeenth-century François Fénelon from Sarlat, who tutored King Louis XIV's son, the Dauphin. Fénelon's spiritual writings helped countless unhappy people: "Eliminate from your daily recreation everything which leads to distraction not necessary to rest your mind..."

Less than an hour away from Fénelon's hometown is Rocamadour, a pilgrimage place since the twelfth century, when the uncorrupted body of a little man was identified as Zacchaeus the tax collector, who climbed a tree to see Jesus. At the museum there, an exhibit commemorates the famous composer Francis Poulenc, whose hands were described by the French writer Colette as "great boney structures that stretched over an octave and a half."

In the busy wine town of Bergerac, a statue of Rostand's Cyrano de Bergerac is surrounded by flowers. Near Lyons, visit the non-denominational monastery in Taizé where people come searching for answers where a pilgrim said, "First I loved the music [of Taizé] because I play the flute. Now I understand young people need God. This is the time we must decide about life, so we need calm inside."

The Albert Schweitzer Museum in Kaysersville displays photographs of Schweitzer, famous organist and African missionary, in his converted chicken-coop hospital.

Journey through the French Alps with the Busy Body as she follows the footsteps of seventeenth-century St. Francis de Sales, patron saint of writers. "The Holy Spirit does not abide in a house where there are sharp retorts, bickering, and arguments."

Follow Giuseppe Garibaldi (born in Nice) through Italy, Sardinia, and Sicily as he fights with his famous "Redshirts" to unite Italy. "There is something very attractive in the unassuming simplicity of Garibaldi's character: a total lack of affectation, conceit, or vanity." (Alfred, Lord Tennyson)

The author and her new friends from Sicily

In Memoriam

Pham Viet Tuyen
Martin Sokolowsky
Father Raymond DeVille, Superior Général
Compagnie des Prêtres de Saint Sulpice
and
Danielle Habitzreiter, Artist

Dedicated to

My children who have given me so much love:
Clancy, Steve, Marty, Alan

HEARTFELT THANKS

To the Holy Ghost,
St. John the Evangelist, St Francis de Sales,
and
Our Lady of Victory

Special thanks to Julie, who arranges itineraries, reads maps, counts money, makes reservations, and drives through mountains and streets so narrow we have to take the side mirrors off—and who edits!

And to editorial assistant Sheila Ledenham, for her endless patience and perseverance, and to my long-suffering computer girl, Nancy Sutton.

Acknowledgments

To All My Good-Natured Library Friends

PREFACE

To forget one's ancestry
Is to be a brook without a source,
A tree without a root.

Chinese Proverb

An interest in history goes hand in hand with concern for people. Caught in the isolation of huge apartment complexes, bureaucracies that ignore us, statistics, and opinion polls, it is only natural to turn to faces of human beings who have lived, suffered, and loved.

History gives students a glimpse of life's experiences while nourishing their imaginations. History allows them to identify with other human beings, to admire, fear, and love them. History teaches life.

Regine Pernoud,
Founder and Director,
Centre Jeane d'Arc in Orléans

The Franco-American National Museum of Blérancourt

Famous dead people had bodies that ached, their love lives were traumatic, and many suffered injustice. You feel sorrier for them than you do for yourself. They also make you laugh. The first time Truman Capote saw Venice, he said it was like eating a box of chocolate-covered cherries all at once. When the reporter Robert Benchley first saw Venice, he wired his newspaper editor, "The city is wonderful, but the streets are covered with water. Send instructions."

The Busy Body introduces you to fun details of the past that we all can relate to. Read on. You will make friends with her famous dead people.

CONTENTS

PART I:
The Basque Country

PART II:
France

PART III:
Sardinia And Sicily With Guiseppe Garibaldi

PART IV:
Garibaldi's Freedom Campaigns
1836-1870...34 Years!

The Basque Country and France

PART I

THE BASQUE COUNTRY

1

THE BASQUE COUNTRY
AND GUERNICA

*This extraordinary people preserved their
ancient language, genius, laws, government, and manners
longer than any other nation in Europe.*

—JOHN ADAMS

THIS TRIP BEGAN in the Spanish Basque Country. In Spain, we traveled from Santiago de Compostela to Guernica to find the oak tree where Basque independence began. No one knows the origin of the Basque language, and their land is smaller than New Hampshire. They have been fighting since at least 218 B.C. to keep their independence. In the beginning, there was no formal code—only ancient customs.

When Romans under Pompey conquered Spain in 218 B.C., they allowed the Basques to keep their laws (*fueros*). Visigoths from the Danube conquered both Rome and Spain in the fourth century, and ruled Spain for four hundred years. They were Christians, of a sort, who had converted to Catholicism. Pamplona had an archbishop during the third and fourth centuries. Under the Romans and Visigoths, the Basques became the most devout Christians in Europe.

Muslim Moors conquered the Visigoths in 711 A.D., and the Basques lived side by side with them in a complicated relationship for eight hundred years. In 778, when Charlemagne marched in, his troops were defeated, and in the twelfth century, the Basques put their legal code into writing. After the Basques agreed to live under the kings of Castile (including Ferdinand and Isabella), each king was obliged to stand under the oak tree near their church and pledge support for Basque laws. In 1826, a neoclassic meeting house was built, and in 1860, when the three-hundred-year-old tree died, it was immediately replaced. We found the tree and the meeting house (now a museum) with beautiful mosaic murals of Basque history and a gorgeous stained glass ceiling depicting their treasured oak tree. From the Middle Ages until the French Revolution, Basque leaders met under the tree, but the Revolution changed that. They lost their 250-year-old laws, and were forced to pay taxes to the French government and serve in the revolutionary army.

Napoleon allowed them to continue their meetings but he changed their outdated laws, banned their language, and burned their churches and monasteries. After Napoleon, the Spanish Legislature passed anti-clerical laws to destroy their independence and religion, which was pro-family and anti-communist. The Basques lost two wars against the Spanish government.[1] However, like the Baltic people under Communism, whose Singing Revolution brought about their freedom, the Basques, too, resorted to their ancient folk songs and sang loud and long in their native language of Euskera.

In 1895, on the feast day of their famous saint, Ignatius Loyola, they founded the Basque National Party, an underground independence movement. They composed a national anthem and designed their national flag: a red background representing the people, a green 'X' for the ancient laws and a huge superimposed white cross representing Christ's purity.

---

[1] The Carlos Wars of 1833 and 1872.

Sacred Oak Tree of Guernica

At the beginning of the twentieth century, Karl Marx was writing *Das Kapital* and Alexander Bell had invented the telephone. Times were changing. The early Basques were farmers, sailors, and fishermen whose laws favored them, but later, many Basques were becoming wealthy as shipbuilders and traders. Socialists and Marxists, who wanted a strong, centralized government, infiltrated to divide and conquer by class warfare against "capitalists." Basque extremists joined them, resulting in a bloody three-year civil war (1936–1939).

In 1936, thirty-three-year-old Jose Aguirre, the new Basque leader, took an oath under the oak tree at Guernica:

Humbly before God
Standing on Basque soil
In remembrance of Basque ancestors
Under the Tree of Guernica, I swear
To faithfully fulfill my commission.

At the same time, Hitler and Mussolini, in league with Spanish General Franco, were sending troops, weapons, and planes to bomb Basque towns. Refugees fled to Guernica. On April 2, 1937, when the marketplace was packed with farmers and refugees, German and Italian planes dropped incendiary bombs on the square, killing 1,745 innocent people. Another thousand were injured. Three days later, Franco's troops occupied the town, and eighty thousand orphans had to be evacuated to other countries. The meeting hall and sacred oak tree remained untouched. In response to the bombing of Guernica, Picasso painted his famous painting, *Guernica*, depicting the gruesome tragedy of war and the suffering of individuals.

SANTIAGO DE COMPOSTELA (FIELD OF STARS)

We flew to Madrid and drove from there to Santiago. We cheated. Since the Middle Ages, pilgrims have walked here from all over Europe and still do—with painful blisters—through mountains, rain, snow, and icy winds to visit the tomb of St. James the Apostle, the fisherman. In the twelfth century, one pilgrim warned against thieves, wicked innkeepers, and wolves: "Also going to the torturer of the damned are the fiends who make two compartments in a wine barrel and put different kinds of wine in each. They offer a sample of the better wine but sell the poor wine." He also warned about man-eating packs of wolves so dangerous the archbishop declared, "Every Saturday except Easter and Pentecost, priests, knights, and peasants shall dedicate themselves to the work of hunting wolves. Each church shall supply iron pikes. Anyone who does not help in the hunt shall pay a fine."

There were so many piles of empty scallops[2], brought sixteen miles from the sea for food, that pilgrims returned home with a shell emblazoned with a red cross as a badge of their pilgrimage. Today thousands are still walking "The Way" from all over Europe, loaded down with heavy backpacks and rain gear. Some have walked over five hundred miles. There are four pilgrimage routes through France and Spain and more than 350 rest stops, or *paradors*, on The Way, where papers are stamped providing proof of their journey.

A friend in Santiago who teaches chemistry at the university met us in the garden of our perfect hotel[3] and gave us a tour. Although the famous University of Santiago is located here, the main attraction is the cathedral where St. James is buried. Inside the enormous cathedral, built to house thousands of pilgrims, we stood in a short line and climbed a few steps behind the altar to visit St. James' relics in a silver casket. We missed the noon Mass where six men pull ropes to swing a huge, silver censer hanging from the ceiling to offer incense to God during the Consecration; maybe it was also designed to circulate air from the smell of thousands of stinky pilgrims. At a restaurant near the enormous cathedral, our friend made sure we ate *Tarta de Santiago,* a delicious almond cake. We kept him out so late—long after dark—that his wife called on her cell phone to ask, "Where are you?"

Santiago de Compostela is in the Spanish Basque Country near the Bay of Biscay. In 813 A.D., a hermit in the Spanish province of Galicia followed a path of stars that ended in a place now called Compostela, or "Field of Stars." Under weeds, vines, and shrubs, the hermit found a marble sarcophagus containing the body of a man who, years later, was proven to be St. James the Apostle.

After Christ's Crucifixion and Ascension, the Apostles left to spread the gospel in other lands. St. James went to Spain, but he didn't have much luck with conversions. Returning to the Holy Land, he was killed by King Herod Agrippa at the age of forty-two.[4] Seven disciples rescued his body and placed it in a boat that sailed from Jaffa. Miraculously, they landed on a beach at Padron, off the coast of Spain near Finisterre, or "End of the Land."

---

[2] In France, scallops on the menu are called Conquilles St. Jacques.
[3] Hotel Costa Vella.
[4] In 44 A.D.

Proud Pilgrim with Scallop Shell

A tomb was provided by a noblewoman whose castle and estates were nearby. She ordered two oxen to pull a wagon carrying the sarcophagus to a burial site where they laid St. James to rest. Many wild animals were subdued along the way. The woman was so impressed that she gave her own marble tomb as a sepulcher and was converted to Christianity. St. James' disciples traveled throughout Spain as missionaries, but two remained to guard the tomb. In 1105 A.D., King Alphonse II dedicated a little chapel over the place where St. James was found and where miracles had occurred. Today's famous cathedral is on that site. It was officially recognized in 1884 when, during scientific explorations of the tomb, a pattern in the pavement behind the altar revealed the bones of three men.

The Basque Country was the home of the family of Simon Bolivar (1783–1830), the great liberator of South America. They lived near the Vizcaya coast road before leaving for Venezuela. Two famous missionaries were also from the Basque Country: Ignatious Loyola and Francis Xavier.

IGNATIUS LOYOLA (1490–1556)

Ignatius Loyola was from a Basque warrior family that had fought for Spanish kings for generations and were rewarded with land, wealth, and titles.[5] He was the youngest[6] of eleven children—three sisters and seven brothers. His mother died when he was ten. He was brought up as a page at the court of Ferdinand and Isabella, and became as dissolute as the rest of the courtiers.

In a battle against the French at Pamplona, a cannonball smashed his leg. Three agonizing operations were required. The first was performed by a French surgeon. After the operation, he was sent home to the Loyola castle—thirty miles away—in a litter. The painful trip took six days. The wound didn't heal and required a second excruciating operation by a Spanish surgeon. This time, the bone wasn't set right. It stuck out and, during a third operation, was sawed off.

Helpless for months, he read about knights, chivalry, and saints. He was especially impressed by twelfth-century Saint Francis of Assisi. No longer a ruthless killer who had committed every sin there was, he decided to become a soldier of Christ and a knight for the Blessed Virgin. When his leg healed—although one leg was shorter than the other, and he limped—he made a pilgrimage to the shrine of Our Lady of Montserrat near Barcelona to confess his sins and dedicate himself to God. He wore sackcloth, left his sword and dagger at Our Lady's Altar, and wrote notes for his "Spiritual Exercises."[7] He stayed in a cave at nearby Manresa—fasting and praying for two years—then began eight years of study. In Alcala and Salamanca, where he had gathered a few

---

[5] In Spain, in Azpeitia near Pamplona, a basilica is named for him.
[6] His oldest brother accompanied Columbus on his second voyage.
[7] 200 pages of prayers and meditations.

followers, he and his friends were imprisoned[8] in chains and beaten by the Inquisition for teaching the Gospel and Ten Commandments. He was a "suspect" because he hadn't received his diploma. Released, since "no error was discovered," he packed his books on a donkey and walked to Paris, where he studied at the College of Ste. Barbe (Ste. Barbara)[9] at the famous University of Paris (which consisted of six colleges). One of the theology instructors was a fellow Basque, the future Saint Francis Xavier, who laughed at Loyola's vow to practice poverty and chastity. After two years of friendly debates, Loyola won him over. He wrote that Xavier was "the roughest clay he ever had to knead." At Montmartre, Loyola and six others, including Francis Xavier, took vows of poverty and chastity in a ninth-century crypt. [10]

After graduating in 1534 at the age of forty-three, he returned to Spain, where he worked in a hospital at Azpeitia, caring for the sick. A year later, he joined his companions in Venice, where they were all ordained[11]—except for Pierre Favre, who was already a priest. To fulfill a vow to make a pilgrimage to Jerusalem, he sailed from Barcelona to Jaffa, and from there, rode on a donkey to Jerusalem. When he arrived, Franciscan monks in charge of the Holy Places wouldn't allow him to enter because the Muslims who had conquered Jerusalem were holding Christians hostage for ransom. On his return to Rome, where the streets were filled with frozen bodies dead from cold and starvation, he met Xavier and the others. They took in more than four hundred homeless souls.

In Rome, they obtained permission from Pope Paul III to be ordained, and were given permission to start a new religious order, "The Society of Jesus." They added obedience to their vows and dedicated themselves to the pope. Their motto was, "For the greater glory of God." From a little room in Rome, Loyola sent two or three together around the world to save souls. After years of excruciating stomach pains, Ignatius Loyola died. A huge church in Rome is name for him.

---

[8] Six weeks in Alcala and three weeks in Salamanca.

[9] Endowed by King John III of Portugal.

[10] On a level below the Basilica of Sacre Coeur, a sign that says, "Saint Pierre," points to the left.

[11] At Our Lady Della Salute in the old church next to the hospital.

ST. FRANCIS XAVIER (1506–1552)

Like Loyola, Francis Xavier was from a noble family in the Spanish Basque Country. He was the sixth child. The Xavier castle fortress was near Pamplona, capital of a little kingdom, Navarre, that had been independent for three hundred years. When King Ferdinand incorporated Navarre into the kingdom of Aragon in 1511, the Xavier family was ruined.

At nineteen, Xavier went to study at the University of Paris. He was a twenty-four-year-old professor of theology when crippled, thirty-eight-year-old Loyola arrived and was assigned as his roommate. Another roommate was the priest Pierre Favre, a shepherd from the Savoy region. After the three roommates and four others dedicated themselves to Christ, Xavier's first overseas assignment was in India. He left with two others from Lisbon, Portugal. After thirteen months at sea, they landed[12] in Goa,[13] which had been ruled for thirty-two years by the Portuguese who had married Hindus and built churches, a cathedral, and convents. "Morning crowds went to purchase slaves. Girls from all parts of India were put up for sale ..." Xavier wrote. "The suffering of the native people from one another and from the Portuguese made a permanent bruise on my soul."

He lived at the hospital and heard confessions of galley slaves and convicts, but spent most of his time with the sailors with whom he could relate—waves sweeping over the deck, sun madness, salted fish that coated their tongue and throats with ulcers, and water so polluted they had to cover their mouths with cloths. On Sundays, he said Mass for lepers outside the city. He stayed in GOA five months, then left to visit coastal villages.[14] In CAPE COMORIN, pearl fishers with knives in their mouths died early from asthma, a result of diving underwater for such a long time. He brought two interpreters to teach the natives about the Virgin Mary, Joseph, and Baby Jesus—born in a manger, who died on a cross to save and help His people. He walked through streets in his cassock, carrying an umbrella and ringing a bell to collect a crowd (of mostly women and children). He taught them to

---

[12] May 6, 1542.

[13] Headquarters for fifteen cities held by the Portuguese, around the southern coast of India.

[14] Where the people were called *Paravas*.

sing the Credo, and they loved the Baptismal ceremony—even though they didn't understand a word. He walked a hundred and fifty-five miles from CAPE COMORIN on the coast to the seaport of COCHIN (today's KOCHI, in the state of Kerala), through mountains infested with tigers, jackals, and snakes—"a hot Asiatic oven."

He also walked to today's CHENNAI (formerly MADRAS),[15] to a part of the city called MYLAPORE, to pray at the tomb of St. Thomas the Apostle (the Doubting Thomas who was martyred there in 52 A.D.[16]). It was a miracle he got out of the MALACCA Islands alive. Headhunters ate the soft flesh of women and children. They knew every poison, and they used them. Xavier wrote that they put cloves in everything: medicine, cooking, and perfume. On the small volcanic island of MALACCA (where Muslim pirates cut off the noses, ears, and feet of native fishermen), Xavier met a Japanese nobleman, Anjiro, "a soul without God," who became a convert and accompanied him to Japan. They left for Japan from GOA, but stopped at COCHIN and MALACCA.

They landed at the harbor town of KAGOSHIMA, Anjiro's island village. Xavier stayed a year with Anjiro's family, who introduced him to important people, but he made few converts. Soon the novelty of meeting a foreigner wore off, and he left for HIRADO, an inland port. Again, the two men walked for two weeks. In HIRADO, Xavier stayed with a samurai[17] and his family at their palace, but the return trip to KAGOSHIMA was a nightmare. Mountains and valleys were covered with snow up to their knees. They forded icy streams, ate only fried rice, and were driven from inns and stoned by children.

At YAMAGUCHI, where they preached on corners and begged for food, a Chinese merchant rescued them. He cleaned them up and gave them food, clothes, and a mattress to sleep on. He introduced them to prominent people, including a man who arranged a meeting with the Daimyo, the "Lord of the Land." Through Xavier's Japanese interpreter, Anjiro, they discussed travel and religion, but when Xavier criticized the Japanese practice of sodomy, the furious Daimyo ordered them out of the palace. Xavier's companion wrote, "I myself was afraid he would take off our heads."

---

[15] In the State of Kerala at that time it was KYOKO. Today, KYOTA.

[16] According to Marco Polo, he was venerated by both Christians and Muslims.

[17] A warrior of the military aristocracy.

On his first trip to KYOTA (the Imperial City), the residence of emperors for more than a thousand years, he preached in the street against women who killed their children at birth and even before. In the homes of nobles, he spoke of Lucifer and "The Fall of the Angels" (who were cast into hell for their sin of pride), but the Japanese didn't want to think about their ancestors being in hell. His visit was a total failure, but he was determined to return—and he did.

The second time, they got lost. A wealthy merchant pitied them when he saw them begging in the street. He took them in and told them that the Daimyo was the most powerful warrior of the empire—more powerful than the emperor, the Mikado. The only way to enter the palace was to disguise themselves as servants to a prince. Xavier and his companion dressed themselves in the magnificent clothes they had intended to give to the emperor (silk robes, gold turbans, and brocaded gloves). Xavier, now disguised as Lord Francis, with a dapper secretary and two servants carrying their luggage, walked into the palace behind a prince in his elegant litter.

The palace doors opened promptly, and guess who the Daimyo was? The same Daimyo who had thrown them out the door at YAMAGUCHI. The Daimyo couldn't believe that the splendid courtiers were the same people he had met before, especially when they presented him with wonderful gifts: a clock that struck the hours, a music box, a mirror, a three-barreled musket, and two pairs of spectacles. Impressed, he granted Xavier's every wish. He authorized him to teach the Christian religion, and even gave him a monastery and a little palace. Xavier showed his converts religious paintings and taught them to sing their prayers. Like the Pied Piper, the children tagged behind him.

Returning to GOA, he learned he had been appointed administrator for all Jesuit missions in the Indies and beyond—which meant Japan and China. After putting his affairs in order, he sailed for China, which was closed to foreigners. The captain of the ship (the Santa Cruz), was in unfamiliar waters, and Xavier took over as pilot. He landed November 22, 1522, six miles from the mainland at SANCIAN, a small island filled with Portuguese smugglers. While waiting for someone to smuggle him into Canton, he came down with a high fever (malaria). This time his companion was a Chinese convert named Anthony, who rowed him out into a rough sea at night to the ship still in the harbor. But after being thrown around in the boat by icy Siberian winds, he asked to be brought back to shore. The once handsome champion high-jumper at the University of Paris, known for his beautiful smile, was now forty-six, emaciated, and had white hair. In a little hut made of fronds, he died December 3, 1522. Anthony again rowed out to the ship to inform the captain. Xavier's incorrupt body was brought to MALACCA and, eventually, to GOA, where he was buried in the Basilica of The Good Jesus. His fellow Basque missionary, Ignatius Loyola died four years later. They both died while English King Henry VIII was getting rid of his wives.

From Spain, we followed the pilgrims' route through Pied de Port, Burgos, San Sebastian, and up the coast to Calais in France, where Général de Gaulle was married. Then on to Lille, his birthplace, and Reims to visit the impressive World War II Museum, with photographs, newspaper headlines, and uniforms[18] depicting "the way it was"—lest we forget.

---

[18] Especially General Patton's tailor-made uniforms.

PART II

FRANCE

2

PARIS

THE FIRST DAY in Paris we got lost. We ended up at St. Sulpice[19] instead of St. Germaine des Prés, and dined at an outdoor restaurant near rue des Canettes, where the Three Musketeers fought their famous duel with d'Artagnan (after one of them laughed at his old yellow pony "without a hair on its tail"). We had no idea how to find our hotel on rue St. Jacques. The owner of the restaurant walked us up streets and around corners in the dark until—*voilà!* Our hotel.

We crossed off all the places on our list, including churches associated with St. Vincent de Paul, who had been chaplain to galley slaves under Kings Louis XIII and Louis XIV. Another church was St. Denis de la Chapelle, where Joan of Arc prayed before being wounded in an attempt to retake Paris from the English. St. Augustine's Church,[20] and many others, have little parks around them with flowers, benches, and play areas. Everywhere, roses bloomed for us.

Musée Grévin on Boulevard Haussmann was another "must," with wax figures representing French history. The sound and light

---

[19] One of the oldest parishes in Paris. Begun in 1494, the tradition of church music started here with famous Couperin family of organists (for 175 years).

[20] Named for St. Augustine, born in today's Algiers. He wrote *City of God* when Rome was captured by Alaric the Hun in 410.

show, with four thousand bulbs, included a tropical storm, a cave scene, and Balinese dancers! We climbed the Eiffel Tower, patted gargoyles atop Nôtre Dame, checked out the Opêra Museum, and spent hours in the Science Museum. Then peace, quiet, and beauty at Parc des Buttes-Chaumont, once a chalk quarry landscaped on many levels by Napoleon III and Georges Haussmann.

A friend (a Paris tour guide from Bulgaria who speaks seven languages) met us at a café near Hôtel de Ville, where an enormous television screen had been set up to watch the Coup de Monde soccer game at 5:30 p.m. Her problem at the moment involved Russians, Bulgarians, and people from New Zealand who had paid for soccer tickets which were nonexistent. She brought me a piece of wood from Lafayette's ship, *L'Hermoine*, which is being reconstructed at Rochefort. After she left to comfort a group of disgruntled Italians, we attended a most unusual church service at St. Gervais–St. Proteus (Roman martyrs) behind Hôtel de Ville. For nearly an hour, twenty monks in white hooded robes, nuns in grey, and young laymen and women knelt in front of the altar in silent prayer. Outside, Paris seethed with people and buses, but not a sound could be heard. Mass began with beautiful music: harmonized singing from the Book of Psalms accompanied by a guitar and viola. All of Paris is their monastery.

One of the best restaurants in Paris was Le Pocquelin,[21] named for the father of Molière,[22] who lived across the street on rue Richelieu. Our timing for dinner was perfect. The proprietors, Maggy and Michel Guiollaumin, were retiring after twenty-eight years as owners. The handsome chef was their son, Benoît. The next day, we cruised leisurely down the scenic St. Martin Canal, lined with leafy chestnut trees where families were picnicking. We left from Parc de la Villette,[23] went through nine double locks and a tunnel under Place de la Bastille, then docked at Pont de l'Arsenal near the Musée d'Orsay.

---

[21] Today it is a Sushi bar.
[22] Author, playwright, and producer under King Louis XIV.
[23] Where the largest Science Museum in Europe is located.

CHURCHES AND LOUIS BRAILLE
St. Étienne du Monts and Ste. Geneviève

Near the Pantheon, the Church of Saint Étienne[24] du Mont contains the shrine of Sainte Geneviève. When Attila the Hun, the terror of Europe, was headed toward Paris with seventy thousand warriors in the fifth century, fifteen-year-old Geneviève promised Parisians if they would pray to God and not flee, Attila would not harm Paris. Their prayers were answered. Instead of sacking Paris, Attila veered off toward Orléans (451 A.D.).

When King Childeric, leader of the Franks, blockaded Paris, Geneviève led a convoy up the Seine to Troyes and returned, undetected, with food for the starving people. King Childeric even released prisoners of war at her request. Childeric's son, King Clovis, was a convert to Christianity; he built a church (later destroyed) dedicated to Saint Stephen over Geneviève's tomb, and made her Patroness of Paris. The cornerstone was laid by the first wife of Henri IV, "the lady's man." The delicate, lacy rood screen[25] is the only one in Paris. Playwright Racine and Blaise Pasçal (writer and inventor of the barometer, syringe, calculating machine, etc.) were buried from here. Sunday Masses are at 9:30 a.m. and 11:00 a.m.

St. Séverin (The University Church)

In the Latin Quarter on the Left Bank, a sixth-century church was built over the tomb of a pious hermit named Séverin. The present fifteenth-century Gothic church on rue des Prêtres near the Sorbonne was dedicated to St. Maurice, martyred in 507 A.D. During the Revolution, ammunition was stored here. To win support, Napoleon returned the building to the Church. Some churches are forgettable, but not this one—especially the majestic palm tree columns. Famous for its concerts, the church has always used beauty in music and art to praise God.

---

[24] Stephen.
[25] An altar screen separating the altar from the rest of the Church.

Julien Le Pauvre (The Poor Man)

St. Julien Le Pauvre, near St. Séverin, is named for a nobleman who, through mistaken identity, killed his parents. In expiation for his crime, he went with his wife to live by a ford in a river. One day, they rescued a man—nearly frozen to death[26]—who told Julian that Jesus had forgiven him. The stranger transformed into a radiant angel and suddenly vanished. The church was built as a chapel in the sixth century. The present church was started in the twelfth century (the same time Nôtre Dame Cathedral was being built) with one hundred monks. Julien le Pauvre was once the official seat of the newly chartered University of Paris, the Sorbonne.[27] In 1889, it was given to the Melchites, the Eastern Catholic Church. All the services are sung in Greek. The dark, intimate church, with six rows of icons, has a special aura of sanctity.

St. Germain du Près

Near the cafés Flore and Les Deux Magots in the Latin Quarter, the site of the sixth-century St. Germain Church was once a meadow (*les prés*) cultivated by Benedictine monks. Pope Alexander III consecrated it a few days before laying the cornerstone for Nôtre Dame. After recovering from four Viking raids in forty years, the church prospered. During the French Revolution, three hundred monks were killed. The library was destroyed and the church used as a factory to make cannon powder.

Today, in addition to medieval sculpted eagles, lions, and pelicans, the church has wonderful concerts and contains the tomb of René Descartes (the father of analytical geometry), who moved to Sweden to found a "School of Learning" for Queen Christina.

St. Nicolas du Chardonnet

On a Sunday morning while wandering near the Pantheon, I asked a good-looking blonde lady who appeared to be in her forties where I

---

[26] Rue Galande. A sculptured stone depicts St. Julien and his wife rowing their stranger across the river.

[27] Named for Robert Sorbon, confessor to King Louis IX (St. Louis).

should go to Mass. The friendly lady, Louise, told me to come with her to nearby St. Nicolas du Chardonnet (thistle). I don't know the secret of its success, but the church was packed. A long procession of innocent young children in red and white robes carried lighted candles down the aisle. During Mass, the church resounded with devout parishioners singing beautiful French hymns and responses.

Val de Grâce

The church and convent of Val de Grâce, located on the Left Bank, was commissioned by Louis XIV's mother, Anne of Austria, in thanks for the birth of her first child after twenty-two years of marriage to religious Louis XIII—the one under Cardinal Richelieu's thumb. The convent, administered by Benedictine nuns, was built in 1645, during the time of Rubens, Brueghel, and Galileo.

My visit was not exactly a waste of time—at least I found it— near rue de la Harpe and Jardin des Plantes, but the receptionist said the only way to visit the queen's apartment, chapel, and garden was with a tour group. She also said that since 1793, the buildings, including the chapel, have been used as an Army Medical Hospital. I was as disappointed as Louis's XIV's mother must have been with her son, who thought he was the Sun King and could do no wrong.

Nôtre Dame Cathedral

The whole world meets at Nôtre Dame Cathedral. It is where people come to light candles, a flame of hope in the dark; where wanderers come home to Mary, God's mother who understands; where Napoleon (1804) snatched the emperor's crown from Pope Pius VII and crowned himself; and where an English king (Henry VI) was crowned king of France.

Pope Alexander III laid the foundation for Nôtre Dame in the twelfth century (1163–65). The gargoyles on the roof were supposed to drive away evil spirits, but they must have been asleep during the French Revolution. Above the front portal, the crazed mob chopped the sculpted heads off twenty kings of Judah and six kings of Israel. They thought they were French. After the Revolution, the publication of Victor Hugo's *The Hunchback of Nôtre Dame* resulted in badly-needed repairs. During World War I, the cathedral was used as a wine warehouse for military hospitals, sparing it from destruction. During the latter days of World War II, the cathedral was saved when German General Choltitz disobeyed Hitler's order to destroy the entire city. Bombs planted beneath the cathedral were ready for a Nazi signal.

The Madelèine (Magdalen)

This is the famous church with fifty-two marble columns and twenty-eight steps where tour buses park. Originally, Napoleon wanted a Temple of Glory built here to honor his French Army, but, after Waterloo, that wasn't such a good idea. King Louis XVIII, who had fled during the Revolution, decided it should be a church in memory of King Louis XVI and members of his family: Marie Antoinette, their son, and the king's sister, Mme. Elizabeth.

The church was completed during the reign of Louis Philippe, the "Citizen King," and consecrated to Mary Magdalene. Carved on each side of the front door are the Citizen King's patron saints, St. Louis and St. Philippe. St. Louis died on a pilgrimage, and St. Philippe is the apostle who, during the Last Supper, said, "Lord show us the Father." Christ didn't say, "You're looking at Him." Instead, he said, "I am in the Father, and the Father is in me" (John 14:9, 11). The ears of corn, olives, and bunches of grapes carved on the church door signify the bread, wine, and oil used in the sacraments.

When we saw people going through a door to the left of the altar, we followed them down into a crypt where the remains of a parish priest killed during the Commune[28] are buried. Chopin's funeral was here, and St. Saëns and Fauré were church organists.

---

[28] 1871 Civil War.

Sacre Coeur and Montmartre (Hill of Martyrs)[29]

After the Prussians defeated France in 1870, they occupied Versailles. In the Peace Treaty, the National Assembly gave away Alsace-Lorraine, in addition to a huge war settlement. Revolutionaries wanted to continue the war, but the government settled for peace at any price. Bismarck and the Prussians at Versailles noted the beginning of a civil war[30] of hate and revenge between the Commune revolutionaries and the government. Parisians, surrounded and starved by the Prussians, ate most of the animals in the zoo. The only way to communicate with the provinces was by carrier pigeons and primitive balloons with highly explosive coal gas—and no compass.[31]

After shelling Paris for three weeks, Foreign Minister Bismarck and the Prussians left Versailles, leaving the Monarchists and Communards to kill each other. To prevent the anti-church, anti-private property Commune[32] from taking over the government, the National Assembly went to Versailles while the Communards unfurled their red flag and set up their own government at the Hôtel de Ville.

The slaughter began at the top of Montmartre when the outnumbered Communards attacked the National Guard troops and were defeated. In retaliation, the Communards killed two generals, a much-loved doctor, fifty hostages, and the archbishop of Paris, Monsignor Darboy.[33] Government troops bombed Paris for six weeks, followed by a week of vicious street fighting. The massacre ended after government troops killed the remaining one hundred forty-seven Communards. Between twenty thousand and thirty-six thousand Parisians died. In reparation or contrition to the Sacred Heart of Jesus (*Sacré Coeur*), a basilica was built at the top

---

[29] St. Peter's Chapel on Montmartre, where Ignatius Loyola took vows that led to the founding of the Jesuits (Society of Jesus).

[30] "One does not negotiate with assassins."—Jules Favre

[31] Red Republican leader, Leon Gambetta, fled Paris in a balloon at night in freezing temperatures; bundled up in a fur coat, terrified but determined, he landed in Tours and made himself dictator.

[32] Commune means "those who have something in common."

[33] Also five other priests and fifty hostages. The archbishop's body was found later ripped open by bayonets and dumped into a ditch in Père Lachaise cemetery.

of Montmartre, where the massacres had begun. Visitors sit near the altar to see the mosaic of Christ's outstretched arms. The church is open day and night. Priests talk with visitors, answering questions, and there is an audio–video history of the basilica in the crypt.

Chapel of the Miraculous Medal

During the Revolution of 1830, at 140 rue du Bac in Paris, the Virgin appeared to a lowly nun, Catherine Labouré, who belonged to St. Vincent de Paul's Order of Our Lady of Charity. The Virgin told her, "Have a medal struck according to this model. Those who wear it with faith will receive great graces ..." Today, the miraculous medal is worn by Christians throughout the world. When the Virgin appeared to Bernadette at Lourdes, Bernadette was wearing the medal, inscribed with the prayer, "Mary conceived without sin, pray for us who have recourse to thee."

St. Eustache

Near the Louvre, this sixteenth-century church—one of the most beautiful in Paris—was built for nobility and merchants at Les Halles (once the central marketplace). The church was named for a Roman general, Eustace. After the general's conversion to Christianity in the second century, he, along with his wife and two children, were locked in a bronze bull and burned because Eustace refused to worship idols.

The list of celebrities associated with St. Eustache reads like a *Who's Who* column: King Louis XIII and his Queen, Anne of Austria, were buried from here, along with Molière, Mirabeau, La Fontaine, and Colbert, Prime Minister for Louis XIV. Here, Gounod directed a choral society, Franz Liszt heard his Mass performed for the first time, and Berlioz premiered his *Te Deum*. Molière was originally buried here in a cemetery for unbaptized babies, since actors were not allowed burial in consecrated grounds. Eventually his remains were transferred to Père la Chaise cemetery. Colbert was buried secretly at night to prevent riots; the mob held him responsible for Louis XIV's extravagance and taxes.

St. Germain L'Auxerrois

This church near the Louvre was founded in 500 A.D. as a small private chapel commemorating a visit by the Bishop of Auxerré (near Dijon). Twice the bishop was sent to Great Britain—once to defeat the Pict and Saxon tribes, and fourteen years later to stop monks from preaching against the doctrine of original sin. The little chapel became a baptistry where children were quickly baptized in case they were drowned during floods.

The Torrent and the River

With a mighty rush and road,
Adown a mountain steep
A torrent tumbled,—sweeping o'er
Its rugged banks,—and bore
Vast ruin in its sweep.

—JEAN DE LA FONTAINE

Later the chapel was fortified against the Vikings. Today's beautiful church near the Louvre was commissioned by King Philip Augustus to protect Paris while he and Richard the Lionheart galloped off to the Third Crusade. Molière was married here. Artists, musicians, and architects living in the Louvre were buried from here. One was Adolphe Willette, who drew caricatures for the *Le Chat Noir*,[34] the cabaret's newspaper. In 1885, when the cabaret moved to rue Laval, Willette designed the stained glass window on the first floor.

In 1926, to keep a vow that Willette (a convert) had made, his friends rounded up his artist friends on Ash Wednesday to attend Mass, receive ashes, and pray for those among them who might die during the year. Every year since then, artists renew the ceremony on

---

[34] Black cat.

Ash Wednesday. A pamphlet in the church quotes: "'My house,' said the Lord, 'shall be called a house of prayer for all peoples'" (Isaiah 56:7). It also says, "Paris needs these havens of silence where poets and the needy and lowly can find deep, interior peace."

St. Sulpice

St. Sulpice is named for a seventh-century bishop of Bourges. As you enter the church, you are greeted by an enormous holy water font in the shape of two giant shells, a gift from the Venetians to King Francis I. Then you look up and see the astonishing pulpit, installed in 1789. The priest giving the sermon seems to be floating in the air, standing in a balloon basket anchored on each side by a marble stairway to heaven. Paintings by Delacroix adorn either side of the front door. Moliere's wife, Armande, the baby of the acting troop, was buried from St. Sulpice, and Lafayette's wife, Adrienne, was a parishioner.

Nôtre Dame de l'Assomption [35]
(Our Lady of the Assumption, the Polish Church)

Lafayette's funeral was here. His coffin was draped with the French Tricolor flag and the American Stars and Stripes. No orations or demonstrations were allowed. Citizen King Louis Philippe's government feared Lafayette's ideas. As thousands watched his funeral procession, National Guards policed them to prevent riots against the government.

This church, near my hotel[36] on rue St. Honoré, is the first one I visited in Paris. Preparations were being made for a baptism, but the godparents (a pretty blonde dressed in chic Parisian clothes, and her tall, handsome husband) were having a problem keeping track of their three-year-old son, who was hiding behind pews. I scooped him up and diverted his attention until the ceremony was over. What began as a casual drop-in visit ended in a beautiful friendship and a baptismal party in the suburbs of Montrouge, three miles south of Paris.

---

[35] 263 rue St. Honoré, rue de Chavelier et St. George where a statue of the Polish poet Mickiewicz stands.

[36] Hotel Loti, named for the French naval officer, novelist, and artist.

Église St. Roch (Rock)

As Lafayette and his wife, Adrienne, were about to enter St. Roch for evening vespers, Lafayette was arrested "by order of the king." His sword was taken, his hands tied behind his back, and he was led away like a criminal. His crime? He had gone to America illegally.[37] After the French Revolution, Napoleon fired from the steps of the church into a crowd of Royalists attempting to capture artillery from the newly-formed Republic. In 1841, Alexandre Dumas married the actress Ida Ferrier here. During the ceremony, the priest gave Dumas a lecture, warning him to "Leave behind you those dangerous emotions of the theatre; those perfidious sirens of passion ..."

King Louis XIV (1638–1715) laid the cornerstone of St. Roch, which was named for a fourteenth-century saint from Montpellier who went on a pilgrimage to Rome and ended up in the middle of a plague, where he miraculously cured many victims. When he, too, contracted the plague, a dog cared for him. When he recovered and returned home, his relatives, not recognizing him, had him imprisoned as an imposter. He died in prison. Le Nôtre, the landscape designer, Diderot, editor of the *Encyclopédie*, and portrait painter Pierre Mignard were also buried here.

Ste. Clotilde

Sixth-century Clotilde, daughter of a Burgundian king, married Clovis, king of the Franks. During the reign of Napoleon III, the eldest son of Charles Worth (dress designer for Empress Eugénie) wrote about his father, "Every New Year's day, the first thing he did in the morning was to take us to Ste. Clotilde's to spend three quarters of an hour in silent worship."

Nôtre Dame des Victoires

The small church in Place des Petits Pères is one of the major shrines to the Virgin Mary in France. It was started in 1629 by barefoot Augustinian monks, *Petits Pères*, under the patronage of King Louis XIII. The present

---

[37] He was under house arrest for several weeks.

church was built by King Louis XIII as a promise after a victory at La Rochelle. In 1883, fourteen-year-old St. Thérèse of Lisieux stopped here with her father and sister on their way to Rome to obtain permission for the little girl to enter the Carmelite convent, although the required age was fifteen. In Rome, she grabbed the pope's legs,[38] pleading with him. A papal guard tucked her under his arm and marched her away, but she received permission six days after she arrived home.

St. Nicholas des Champs (Fields) and Louis Braille (1809–1852)

The huge nine-hundred-year-old church is named for a fourth-century bishop of Myra (in Turkey), who became known as Santa Claus. There are so many columns in the church I lost count.

I was lucky to meet a charming lady volunteer on her way out. She kept the church open long enough for me to see the organ that Louis Braille played.

Blinded at three, Braille was enrolled at the Institute for the Blind in Paris at the age of ten by a saintly man, Valentin Haüy, who introduced the boy to Mme. Thérèse Paradis. She opened the world of music to the little twelve-year-old boy, and was responsible for his organ lessons at St. Anne's church.

An ex-army captain, Charles Barbier (who invented a code for signaling troops at night), gave Braille the incentive to invent his Braille system. Braille died of tuberculosis at forty-three[39] before his work was recognized, but one of his blind students,[40] a young girl from Alsace-Lorraine, helped make him famous. She gave piano concerts—attended by wealthy, influential Parisians—using Braille's dot system,[41] and gave all the credit to Braille. At that time in Paris, there were thousands of soldiers who had been blinded during Napoleon's wars. During the Paris Exposition (1898), Emperor Napoleon III introduced and publicized Braille's system of reading for the blind to the world.

---

[38] Pope Leo XIII.

[39] At Couvray, thirty miles from Paris where he was born.

[40] Thérèse Kleinert.

[41] At the age of 15, Braille created a system with six raised dots for the letters of the alphabet. Later he made different codes for math and music.

3

OUTSIDE PARIS

SURESNES
American Cemetery

AT SURESNES, four miles from Paris on the eastern slope of Mont Valerian, we visited the American Cemetery. We took a train from Gare St. Lazare and thought we could take a bus to the cemetery, but there was a problem. Three bus drivers brought us to the American Hospital. We finally took a taxi. The view of Paris from Mont Valerian is awesome. The seven-and-a-half-acre cemetery, once called Mont Calvaire, was the site of a hermitage where hermits maintained gardens, a vineyard, and a retreat guest house. Thomas Jefferson was a frequent guest. Of the 116,516 Americans who died during World War I, 1,541 are buried at Suresnes.

Beautiful Gabrielle Mihaeseu, administrator of the cemetery, told us that during World War II, German troops occupied a fort here, where they executed 4,500 political prisoners and members of the Resistance. A monument dedicated by the French honors them. In a World War II Memorial Room, a plaque says, "In grateful memory of American soldiers, sailors, marines, and airmen throughout the world who sacrificed their lives that others might be free of oppression."[42] A frieze depicts a group of soldiers carrying an empty casket, commemorating the remains of twenty unknown comrades. When I congratulated Gabrielle on her position as Associate at the Memorial Cemetery, she showed us a small, seventeen-year-old newspaper clipping advertising for the job. She won!

Also at Suresnes, there is a street named for Charles Worth. His enormous mansion overlooking Paris is gone, but his son Gaston's villa is used today for offices of "Foundation Foch," a big hospital named for World War I French General Foch.

Charles Worth (1825–1895)

Born in Lincolnshire, England, Charles Worth had to earn a living from the age of twelve. At twenty he came to Paris and worked in a fashion accessory shop.[43] A tailor in the same building had made clothes for Citizen King Louis Philippe, who fled during the 1848 Revolution.[44] Prince Louis Napoleon became president, and Worth married an apprentice in the shop where he worked, a French girl from Clermont-Ferrand.[45]

Louis Napoleon made himself emperor in 1852. During his reign, the Tuileries palace was restored, and railroads, telephones, and canals were introduced. When the department store Bon Marché opened in Paris, Worth designed dresses for his wife to wear at work there. She received so many compliments that Worth was given permission to open a dressmaking department at the store. When Emperor Louis Napoleon married Eugénie from Spain, Worth chose the color rose for her inaugural dress, and Gerlaine invented a perfume for her.

Worth headed the dressmaking department, and his wife modeled his expensive creations. Women's street skirts were made wider, and

---

[42] Eleven World War I American aviators who fought for France in rickety airplanes before the United States entered the war are buried in a Paris suburb at St. Cloud Park. The crypt is marked by a pathetic, dilapidated Arch of Triumph memorial. Their squadron was called Lafayette's Esquadrille. Captain Eddie Rickenbacker's 94th Squadron included many former members of the famed Lafayette Esquadrille. Take the RER and get off at Garches Marnes la Coquette.

[43] Gagelin and Opigez.

[44] His palace was sacked and his throne thrown out a window.

[45] June 1851.

during the Crimean War (1853–1856), while French soldiers were dying under horrible conditions, society ladies wore two new colors for their ballroom dresses: Crimean green and Sebastopol blue. Their dresses, with stiff crinoline petticoats, were draped over a contraption that resembled a parrot's cage. When Worth designed it, he meant it only for one season, but he had created a monster. He hated it, and the ladies loved it.

After the Crimean War, Worth went into business with a partner.[46] They opened their establishment on the rue de la Paix, near Gerlaine's perfume shop. While French soldiers were being slaughtered in Italy, in Paris the new fashion colors were magenta (a pinkish mauve for the battle at Magenta)[47] and bright blue, for the Battle of Solferino.

At thirty-five, Worth enlarged his showrooms and used models to display his designs. One design was inspired when he saw a female street sweeper tying her skirt up over her petticoats to keep it out of the dirt. He still hated the billowing "cage" with petticoats and tightly laced corsets, but that's what the ladies wanted. Their dresses took up so much space, it was impossible not to notice them. Another large department store opened—Le Printemps. By then, Worth had a staff of twelve hundred and a fortune that he spent on his estate at Suresnes:

> The owner of this abode which resembles the interior
> of a kaleidoscope, returns in the evening incapable of eating,
> incapable of enjoying his astonishing and glittering prosperity,
> his nerves on edge by the varied perfumes of the
> great ladies he has been dressing all day.
>
> —THE GONCOURT BROTHERS

One of Worth's favorite acquaintances was brilliant, hard-working Count de Morny,[48] the only one the emperor could count on to tell him

---

[46] Otto Bobergh from Sweden.
[47] France and Sardinia against Austria.
[48] Half brother of Louis Napoleon.
Their mother was Josephine's daughter, Hortense.

the truth. When the count died unexpectedly at fifty-five,[49] Worth had a premonition that he, too, would die on that day.

When Empress Eugénie insisted on setting up a monarchy in Mexico with young Maximilian of Austria as ruler, another fashionable color was introduced, Mexican blue. While the court was enjoying horse racing at Longchamps, word came that Maximilian had been shot by a firing squad and his twenty-four-year-old wife[50] had gone insane. The 1867 Paris Exposition celebrations continued, and then the court adjourned to Biarritz to swim and dance to the music of Johann Strauss's *Blue Danube.*

Worth designed Eugénie's dress when she went to Egypt for the opening of the Suez Canal in 1869, while the emperor stayed home, suffering from excruciating gallstone attacks. Alexandre Dumas, fils, warned that the country was being demoralized from top to bottom, not so much due to the increase of prostitution as from society women becoming as immoral as women of the streets. He prophesied the ruin of the nation. After Prussian foreign minister Otto von Bismarck seized Austrian lands, Parisian ladies wore Bismarck Brown. The next year, after the Franco-Prussian War, Bismarck conquered France, and Parisians starved.

Under the Third Republic, hoop skirts finally disappeared and were replaced by ugly dresses, stiff and straight, with a silly bustle in the back. When Worth's partner retired, Worth's sons Gaston [51] and Jean took over the business. His son Jean wrote, "We loved him enough to take great care not to hurt his feelings by seeming to step into his shoes before our time. Mostly we were successful in saving his pride, for sincere affection is a great teacher to tact." Charles Worth died March 10, the day he dreaded—the day on which Count de Morny had died.

After our visit to Suresnes, we met a friend for dinner who works for Thierry Mugler, the fashion designer. She brought me a bottle of his *Angel* perfume, a gift as precious as a pearl in an oyster—even more: pearls don't smell like Thierry Mugler's *Angel.*

---

[49] March 10, 1865.
[50] Daughter of King Leopold of Belgium.
[51] The Communists tried to enlist Worth's older son, Gaston.

Our last night in Paris was with another friend, a biochemist from Poland. Her husband, Michele, teaches at the Sorbonne, but he was off doing sports of some sort with teenagers. My friend had recently been decorated by the mayor of the suburb, Montrouge, for giving France five children. Also honored were ten blood donors.

PORT MARLEY AND VILLERS COTTERÊTS
Château de Monte Cristo and Alexandre Dumas (1802–1870)

A visit to Alexandre Dumas' dream palace, Monte Cristo, was a must, but it took second place. First, we went to visit friends in Bougival who met us at the train station. They have two little children and two little French cars, a solution for our entourage. Eight people piled into the cars, along with a stroller for two-year-old Emilion and a scooter-bike for feisty, black-eyed, four-year-old Juliette.

On a beautiful summer day, we drove to Port Marly to see Dumas' famous château off the main road from Bougival (where Renoir and the Impressionists hung out at the Fournaise Restaurant), and then on to St. Germaine en Laye. We parked the cars, crossed the road, and followed a winding, shaded path bordered by shrubs and flowers. At the end of the trail, Dumas' Château Monte Cristo stands in the middle of a large courtyard. Opposite, a miniature Renaissance château is surrounded by a moat.

Actually, as châteaux go, Dumas' home is comparatively small, but definitely ornate, with its turrets and towers. A frieze around the outside depicts sculpted heads of geniuses: Homer, Sophocles, Shakespeare, Goethe, Byron, Victor Hugo—and Dumas himself. A broad flight of steps leads to the entrance and foyer. Dumas' motto carved above the stairs says, "*J'aime qui m'aime*" ("I love who loves me"). Practically every actress in Paris loved him—and proved it.

On the first floor, a narrow room is devoted to Dumas' father, who fought with Napoleon. Another room is decorated with stucco arabesques and verses from the Koran, carved by an Arab craftsman and his twelve-year-old son, whom Dumas had brought back from Tunisia. The main salon is white marble and gold, and the second floor has a beautiful view from French windows. Glass showcases contain manuscripts, architectural plans, newspaper caricatures, and sketches from Dumas' books, as well as portraits of his mistresses and children. The library and research center contain his works and private book collection.[52]

While Château de Monte Cristo was under construction, crowds came on weekends to picnic and watch the latest progress. As we wandered through the château with other tourists, I imagined Dumas' rooms filled with mobs of uninvited guests. One time, an unidentified servant bustled around, doing no-one-knew-what. Good-natured Dumas told a friend, "I've stopped him several times and asked him to do some small favors, but he always says, 'Oh Monsieur Dumas. If only I had more than two hands, I would gladly put them at your disposal.'" My daydream was interrupted by excited little Juliet, who had found a pond. "*L'eau! L'eau!*" ("Water! Water!")

Alexandre Dumas' Grandfather

Dumas' grandfather,[53] a nobleman, had a son by a Negress on his plantation in San Domingo, today's Haiti. When the boy's mother died, he came with his father to Villers Cotterêts, fifty miles from Paris. However, when his father married a French woman from Villers Cotterêts, the eighteen-year-old boy (Alexandre Dumas' father) joined the French army as a private and took his mother's last name, Dumas.

Alexandre Dumas' Father

French troops were stationed and billeted at Villers-Cotterêts near Soissons, where the daughter of an innkeeper asked her father's permission to marry a handsome six-foot mulatto with blue eyes, a gentle smile, and crinkly, black hair. It was love at first sight for Marie

---

[52] 1,303 volumes, which include plays, travels, and memoirs.
[53] Antoine Alexandre Davy, Marquis de la Pailleterie.

Louise Labouret. Her father agreed to their marriage only if Dumas advanced to corporal. From corporal, Dumas rose to the rank of general in Napoleon's army, where he was renowned for bravery and the strength of Hercules. During the Egyptian Campaign, Dumas realized Napoleon was sacrificing men, not for France, but for his own glory, and resigned.

The leaky boat in which he sailed back to France had to land in Taranto, Italy,[54] where Napoleon's enemy, King Ferdinand I, ordered Général Dumas jailed and poisoned. Three years later, the former giant of a man was released—blind in one eye, deaf, paralyzed, and crippled—with no income. He hadn't been paid in two years, although he had put down an uprising in Cairo and sent millions in treasure to Napoleon.

Général Murat, Napoleon's brother-in-law and Dumas' comrade-in-arms, sent word to Napoleon about the horrors inflicted on Dumas. A medical officer also pleaded with Napoleon for Dumas' pension. The reply was, "Since you tell me that his health will never again permit him to sleep for six weeks on the desert sand wrapped in bearskin, he is no longer any use to me as a cavalry commander." Général Dumas, commander-in-chief of three armies, died in Villers Cotterêts at forty, leaving his family (a wife and two children—a daughter, Aimé, and four-year-old Alexandre) destitute.

Alexandre Dumas (1802-1870)
The Three Musketeers and *The Count of Monte Cristo*

No doubt about it. There's a magnetism that radiates
from him. A kind of mesmerism. You sense the
showman of freaks and prodigies; the vendor of
wonders, the traveling salesman for the Arabian
Nights. He talks volubly, but what holds you is an
endless array of facts—astonishing facts that he
keeps dredging up in a pleasantly hoarse voice from
memory that is like a bottomless ocean.

—THE GONCOURT BROTHERS

---

[54] In the Apulia region.

Alexandre had worshiped his kind father. His mother and sister taught him to read and write, and a priest taught him a little Latin and grammar, but the only things he was good at were hunting and penmanship.

Napoleon ended up on Elba Island,[55] and gouty King Louis XVIII returned from exile in Ghênt, Belgium. Alexandre's mother secured a license to sell tobacco, and Alexandre, at sixteen and over six feet tall, obtained a job in a notary's office getting local peasants' signatures (X marks) for legal documents—the beginning of his rise to fame, fortune, and misfortune.

While working as a clerk in Villers-Cotterêts, he had met the son of a Swedish nobleman, Adolphe de Leuven, and his friend, Amedée de la Ponce. Amedée told him, "Learn to work and you will find happiness." Dumas' genial response was, "Really? Okay." Amedée also taught him German and Italian. After seeing a troupe of touring actors perform Shakespeare's *Hamlet*, Général Dumas' son knew what he wanted to be—a famous dramatist.

He left for Paris with his friend de Leuven in 1823. En route, they shot rabbits and partridges that they traded for room and board. In Paris, de Leuven arranged for theatre tickets to see the great English actor Talma in *Othello*. De Leuven also arranged a job for Dumas at the Palais Royal, addressing envelopes for the duc d'Orléans, cousin of King Charles X. Dumas' supervisor, Lassagne, assigned him books to read, such as Aeschylus, Schiller, Platus, and Molière, which he memorized. When there was no time to see plays and write his own, he quit his job. The money he earned from a play that he and de Leuven had written equaled three months' salary from the duc d'Orléans.

Catherine Labay, a hardworking, sensible dressmaker, lived on the same floor as Dumas' apartment at #1 place des Italiens. He made love to her and she became the mother of his son Alexandre, known as Alexandre fils to differentiate him from his father (1824). Since marriage did not make sense to the aspiring young playwright, his son and his son's mother were labeled "bastard" and "unwed mother."

---

[55] After Napoleon's defeat, the Congress of Vienna gave Venetio, Tuscany, Parma, Tyrol, and Lombardy to Austria.

After his first successful play,[56] Dumas proudly sent for his widowed mother, who had been worrying about what would become of him. The day before the opening night of *Henri III et sa Cour* (1829), she suffered a stroke that left her right side paralyzed. The play, about Catherine de Medici and her gay son, Henry III, was a tremendous success—the first of Dumas' many historical novels that he adapted.[57] The public clamored for French history à la Dumas. At twenty-seven, he was a wealthy celebrity, writing one hit after another. He made an enormous amount of money and shrugged off jealous critics. "What do you expect of me? I am once and for all simply incapable of hate. Rage? Yes. I can be enraged because it is brief. But hate? I cannot hate. Hate endures."

At Square d'Orléans, he rented an adjacent apartment and invited four hundred people to a costume Artists' Ball. Famous artists climbed on ladders and stools to decorate the walls. Delacroix, with a few quick strokes, painted a whole battle scene. Flowers and two orchestras completed the decor. Dumas' mistress, Belle,[58] acted as hostess. Since the *nouveau riche* host had been given permission to hunt in the Royal Forest of Villers-Cotterêts, the main dinner course was roast deer. One deer was traded for a thirty-pound salmon and a fifty-pound sturgeon. Drinks on the house included three hundred bottles of Bordeaux wine, three hundred Burgundies, and five hundred bottles of champagne. Actors and actresses arrived in costume, straight from the stage door. Lafayette came as a Venetian Doge, Rossini as Figaro, and Delacroix as Dante. Dinner was served at 3:00 a.m., and at dawn they danced in the street.

Belle had a daughter by Dumas named Marie Alexandrine. When Dumas recognized the little girl as legitimate, he remembered he had a seven-year-old son he really should acknowledge. Finally, Alexandre *fils* was recognized as legitimate in 1831. It was about time! Influenced by Belle, his father had denounced his mother, devout Catherine Labay, as an unfit mother. For seven years,

---

[56] His friend, Jules Verne, was a guest in Dumas' private box.

[57] His assistants supplied him with outlines on plans drawn up by Dumas. Then he rewrote the whole thing.

[58] Belle Krebsamer, a Jewish actress from Mulhouse.

abandoned Catherine had supported her son while trying to take time out to play with him. Dumas, whose head was filled with characters, productions, deadlines, creditors, and temperamental actresses, could not handle one more problem, and did as Belle demanded— he applied for custody of the seven-year-old child. The boy was taken from his mother by a police commissioner and put into a boys' boarding school, where bullies subjected the child of an unwed mother to such mental and physical cruelty that his character was affected for life.

While actress Belle was on tour, another actress entered the scene, blonde Ida Ferrier from Strasbourg, who became very fat. She made sure Belle never saw her daughter again. She took over as Marie's mother, and after eight years, in 1840, conned Dumas into marriage (she had bought up all his debts with an ultimatum of marriage or debtor's prison). One night Dumas surprised the best man at his wedding in bed with Ida and threw the lover's clothes out the window. The friend sat shivering naked in a chair while Dumas wrote three newspaper columns for a deadline the next day. When Dumas finally realized his friend was still sitting there, freezing, he apologized and told him to get back into bed with Ida to keep warm.

Dumas' successes continued. Old plays were revived, new ones translated and produced abroad. *Christine,* his second success, was too long. When Christine asked her doctor, "How long before I die?" an exasperated man in the audience yelled, "If you're not dead by 1:00 o'clock, I'm leaving." In his suspense serials, Dumas copied Sir Walter Scott's "to be continued" technique. *Antony*, a melodrama about an adulterous wife, is remembered for the final curtain line, "Dead? Yes dead. She resisted me, so I killed her." The audience went crazy with applause. Today, we would boo and throw popcorn.

In 1830, Paris was flooded with persecuted political émigrés from all over Europe, as well as unemployed Frenchmen and disabled veterans from Napoleon's wars. During the 1830 Revolution, when arrogant, seventy-seven-year-old King Charles X cancelled democratic elections and dissolved Parliament, Parisians revolted, and Charles X abdicated.

Lafayette, commander of the National Guard, needed ammunition, and Dumas volunteered to get it from a powder factory near Soissons—which he did. In an outlandish, red-trimmed uniform of his own design, he marched and drilled in the July heat. He practiced at a shooting range in Vincennes in Paris, while drunken crowds knocked down the altar of Église St. Germain l'Auxerrois and pranced around in the priests' vestments.

Since Paris after the 1830 Revolution wasn't safe for a Republican, Dumas went to the French Alps, Belgium, and Italy under contract to write about his journeys. He returned with a two-volume travelogue, *Impressions de Voyage,* which the public loved. In Florence, he was a sensation but had to write constantly to wipe out debts. He did take a break to visit the island of Elba with Jerome Bonaparte, the son of the ex-king of Naples. A guide suggested a good place to hunt for wild goats and pointed to a cone-shaped island called Monte Cristo rising from the sea.

Back in Paris, Dumas' old boss, the duc d'Orléans, became Louis Philippe, the Citizen King. Algiers was conquered,[59] and in 1832, a cholera epidemic ravaged Paris, taking over seven thousand lives. Every day, fifty to sixty funerals headed for Montmartre Cemetery. Dumas became ill and barely survived. He had asked for a cube of sugar soaked in ether, but his maid gave him half a glass of ether and forgot the sugar. He went into a coma, but recovered after his big body was heated by a bed-warmer filled with hot coals. After recuperating, he left on another assignment to write *Journey Across Two Sicilies.* For his next contract, he went to Switzerland and sent back his *Impressions de Voyage en Swiss*, which was another enormous success. In that five-volume work, readers lived vicariously through him as he wallowed in baths of warm goat's milk and lunched with ex-Empress Josephine's daughter, Hortense.[60]

---

[59] France wanted an Empire again, and sent thirty-seven thousand men in six hundred ships. After five days the Arab governor, the Bey, surrendered. His treasury and artifacts were shipped to France.

[60] Living in exile in Château d'Arenenburg on the shore of Lake Lucerne, five miles west of Constance.

Another success was his novel *Le Capitaine Paul,* which was about John Paul Jones,[61] hero of the American War of Independence. The novel, inspired by James Fenimore Cooper's *The Pilot,* is the true story of a twelve-year-old Scottish boy, whose life was ruined by Russia's Catherine the Great. In 1838, Dumas' bedridden mother, Marie Labouret, died after a second stroke, proud of her "tender, good, and foolish son."

In order to write, write, write, Dumas returned to Florence, where he told his agent, "You know that Paris is a pit. Once you reach the bottom, you do not know how you will get back to the top of the rim. It is seven months that I am climbing with all my strength and I cannot get out."

After partially paying his debts, he could buy on credit again. He rented and renovated Villa Medici, part of the Henri IV Pavilion in St. Germain en Laye.[62] Then he started construction on an enormous theatre with the world's most advanced staging machinery. He also bought six acres of land at Port Marly to build his dream palace. His wife, Ida, left for good to live with a rich Italian nobleman and took Dumas' fourteen-year-old daughter, Marie, with her. Within six months he wrote *Les Trois Mousquetaires* and *Le Comte de Monte Cristo.*[63] Robert Louis Stevenson told about sitting down to read one of Dumas' novels for a long, silent, lamplit evening by a fire. He said it was enlivened with such a clatter of horseshoes, such a rattle of musketry, and such a stir of talk, he still did not know why he should call those evenings "solitary," for he gained so many friends.

In 1844, Dumas went to Spain and Algiers. Before he left, he hosted a party for more than five hundred people on the lawn while his palace was under construction, then took off for Africa. Louis Philip, the Citizen King, had recently defeated the Muslim ruler of

---

[61] To learn more about John Paul Jones, Dumas visited Lorient, where slave ships disembarked.

[62] Still there on rue du Boulingrin.

[63] The idea for the plot came from a case in the police files in Trouville called *Le Diament Dialogue de la Vengeance.* My favorite quote is: "Rogues are preferable to imbeciles because they sometimes take a rest."

Algiers in 1844.[64] Now the French could ship dissidents to Algeria as colonists. Who better than Dumas could advertise the new French territory?

Dumas' Musketeers

The journey began in Spain, where Dumas and his companions[65] attended a royal wedding in Madrid.[66] They were treated like royalty, and a guide escorted them throughout Spain while Dumas wrote nonstop. He took one hundred pages to describe a bull fight. From the Spanish

---

[64] For three hundred years, pirates along the Barbary Coast had been terrorizing traders and demanding protection money. Four years before the 1830 Revolution, the Turkish Bey, in an argument about payment for grain, had slapped the French consul with a fly swatter. French King Charles X waited until June 14, 1830, to declare war on Algiers, the main market for slaves, gold, ivory and ostrich feathers for plumes. He also authorized the French Foreign Legion (*Armé d'Afrique*).

[65] Dumas' *fils* (son), artist Boulenger, and Dumas' valet, Alexia (a little black boy from Madagascar who spoke four languages).

[66] The son of Louis Philippe (the Citizen King), duc de Montpensier, who married Princess Isabella II of Spain.

seaport of Cadiz, they boarded a French gunboat and visited Gibraltar, along with the coastal towns of Tangiers, Algiers, Oran, Tunis, and Tripoli.[67] In Algiers, the conquered ruler, the Bey, welcomed them at his royal fortress, the Kasbah. Dumas published his adventures for over three million readers under two titles, *de Paris à Cadiz* and *Le Volace* (the name of the vessel). On January 3, 1847, they returned to France and another revolution. Dumas barely had time to enjoy the success of his *Théâtre Historique* and finish decorating his château. For a year, he had provided food and lodging for every out-of-work actor, painter, and sponger. One night at dinner, he asked a man seated next to him if he would introduce him to some of the people. The man replied, "I'm a stranger here myself," and poured himself another glass of champagne.

During the six-day revolution in 1848, the destitute people of Paris sacked the Tuileries (the royal palace). Three thousand people died, and six thousand were deported. Dumas' magnificent *Théâtre Historique* folded, and creditors stripped his dream house. After the court declared him bankrupt and reality became too real, he went to Holland to attend the coronation of King Leopold I.[68] Napoleon's nephew, Louis Napoleon, became president of the new Republic, and two years later, in 1851, when he decided to become emperor, the *coup d'état* that dissolved the Legislative Assembly saved Dumas from debtor's prison. Victor Hugo, the emperor's most vocal enemy, had already fled to Brussels. Dumas joined him and other exiles—not for political reasons, but to avoid lawsuits. In Brussels he wrote as if pursued by vengeful Furies—plays,[69] novels, and serials to fulfill contracts. While the exiles gathered in St. Hubert's Passage, Dumas wrote day and night.

His secretary, Noel Parfait,[70] was literally his life preserver. As checks began to come in, he hid the money. Dumas wrote, "I have never been

---

[67] In 1801 pirates betrayed one too many contracts with the new United States. Americans sent warships to attack Tripoli. The victory is immortalized in a line from the U.S. Marine Hymn: "... to the shores of Tripoli."

[68] And his consort, Marie Louise, daughter of Citizen King Louis Philippe.

[69] 1853 *Le Reine Margot* lasted nine hours. Before opening night, people slept outside the Odéon, and vendors sold them bouillon.

[70] Parfait copied Dumas' work in four languages.

so poor since I brought an honest man into the house." As lawsuits were solved and credit restored, off he went on another spending spree. He bought an enormous mansion on blvd. Waterloo and entertained with lavish parties. For one party, he had an Arabian Nights set constructed by the director of the *Théâtre Royal de la Monnaie.* Victor Hugo's son, Charles, wrote from Brussels, "Dumas for the time being is riding pretty in that chariot of fortune which has so often given him a spill." Noel Parfait wrote to his brother about the many loose women with whom he ruined himself.

In Paris after the Crimean War (1856),[71] a Russian friend[72] was leaving for Russia and invited Dumas as his guest. His readers went along too—down the Volga on a nine-month boat trip. According to Dumas, his Astrakhan host, a civil administrator, owned 50,000 horses, 30,000 camels, 10 million sheep, 11,500 tents, and 270 priests. Dumas was entertained at a dinner party where French cuisine was served, and all the guests spoke French. He visited the Tartars as a guest of the Buddha Prince, who owned two thousand peasants and a park thirty miles long. The main course at dinner was filet of horse. In exchange for a shiskabob recipe (roast lamb marinated with a mixture of vinegar and chopped onions), Dumas gave the prince cooking lessons. Dumas, who drank only water, could drink liquor socially if necessary, and more than once left his Russian friends snoring under the table. He wrote to a friend:

> I am writing to you from Kazan on the Volga, the capital of the Tartars. On the map find Elston, a curious salt lake. I camped there in the middle of the steppes and ate mutton from the sea-salted marshes. They served the tail separately. It weighed fourteen pounds. Beds are a completely unknown article of furniture. Parquet floors do not encourage frolicsome thoughts!

---

[71] Russia was now under Tsar Alexander II. In 1840 Dumas had written *Le Maître Armes* about tyranny under Tsar Nicholas I and the Decembrists who had tried to free the serfs long before the Revolution of 1917. The Decembrists were executed or exiled to Siberia, where people were left to freeze in blocks of ice. The book was banned in Russia.

[72] The friend was the son of Count Nesselrode, ambassador to France, whose chef invented Nesselrode desserts—a rum-flavored mixture of chestnuts, preserved oranges, cherries, and dried fruits.

Back in Paris, he published a newspaper, *Les Mousquestaires,* with ten thousand copies in circulation. Famous Parisians contributed free articles. Delacroix said, "He came to see me, notebook in hand. God knows what he's going to do with the details I was so foolish as to give him. I'm very fond of him, but we are as different as chalk from cheese." Dumas wrote constantly, but never saw any money; for one reason, he had made his illiterate ex-gardener the cashier. Applications for new subscriptions ended up in the wastebasket.

When lawsuits were finally settled, he was rich again. He bought a two-masted schooner (the *Emma*), and went to help Giuseppe Garibaldi[73] rescue the Two Sicilies (Sicily and Naples) from the Austrian Hapsburgs and other dictators who were back in power after Napoleon's defeat and the Treaty of Vienna. Dumas had met Garibaldi in Turin a few months before.[74] Among the passengers aboard the schooner were Vasili (Dumas' Russian valet),[75] a doctor, a photographer, his secretary's son, Paul Parfait, and Dumas' nineteen-year-old mistress, Emilie Cordier (another would-be actress), who was dressed as a sailor.[76] Dumas introduced her as his son, but she had to leave for Paris to have a baby.[77] "The boy by day is in the habit of becoming a woman at night."

When Dumas arrived in Marseille in May 1860, he bought arms and furnished two transport ships for Garibaldi's troops. All of Marseille was on the wharf to greet him. His popular novel, *Le Comte de Monte Cristo,* had brought tourists and money to Marseille, especially for the boatmen who took sightseers to the island of d'If to see the hole through which the Count escaped from his prison.

Troop transport ships and arms arrived in Sicily (at Palermo) just in time. An armistice with Neapolitan troops gave Garibaldi a chance to stall—he was out of ammunition. Dumas' dispatches to the Paris

---

[73] Dumas had a grant for a scientific expedition to the Mediterranean coast, but helped Garibaldi instead.

[74] Garibaldi was Dumas' perfect hero.

[75] Dumas had met Vasili in Russia. In 1859, the twenty-year-old youth had made his way alone for two thousand miles to serve Dumas. In Istanbul he had been sick for a month.

[76] Guerlain, the perfumer, sent her perfume and cold cream as a *bon voyage* present.

[77] Emile had a little girl, Micaela, whom Dumas adored.

newspaper *La Press* brought cash contributions from all over the world. In the harbor at Naples aboard the *Emma,* sailors cut and stitched red shirts for Garibaldi's volunteers. When they finished, each sailor left the ship wearing twenty-five shirts on his back to distribute.

After freeing Marsala, Palermo, Milazzo, and Reggio in seventeen days, Garibaldi and his famous "Thousand" volunteers fought their way up to Naples, where they were given a frenzied welcome. Dumas wrote, "I am in Naples where I live in a charming small palace on the shore. All the hunting grounds of François II are at my disposal." As Garibaldi's ambassador, Dumas was appointed Director of Museums and Excavations to continue work that had begun in Pompeii in 1763.

On February 18, 1861—thanks to Garibaldi's Thousand—the king of Sardinia and Piedmont, Victor Emmanuel II, entered Naples and became king of Italy. The island of Sardinia was annexed, and Naples and Sicily were absorbed into the kingdom of Italy. Garibaldi, with no word of thanks, left for his island home, Caprera. "When one has squeezed the juice to the last drop, one throws the orange rind into a corner."

Dumas continued to stay in Naples for four years, writing feverishly.[78] One book, *La Sans Felice,* was about the English naval hero, Admiral Nelson, who defeated Napoleon at Trafalgar. Although married, Nelson met the love of his life in Naples, Lady Hamilton—who was also married. Dumas' novel of their *menage à trois* was a huge success. Another success was *Les Mohicans de Paris (The Savages of Paris),* the first detective story to be staged. It was the first time the phrase '*Cherchez la Femme*' (Search for the Woman) was used. He also published a newspaper, the *l'Independent.* Garibaldi wrote the foreword for the first edition:

> The journal that my friend Dumas is about to start will bear the noble title *The Independent.* It will deserve its name all the more if it attacks me—should I ever turn aside from my principles as a son of the people and a soldier of humanity.

---

[78] He translated Garibaldi's *Memoirs* and Dante's *Divine Comedy* into French, wrote the *History of Naples (Borboni di Napoli), Impressions la Voyage,* and my favorite, *The Black Tulip (La Tulip Noir).*

Dumas returned to Paris with a new mistress, Fanny Gordosa, an Italian singer "with a fragile voice and Vesuvian passions." Dumas tried to promote her, but Fanny was a flop. When she fired the cook and all the servants right before twenty guests arrived, Fanny had to go.

Dumas started another newspaper and wrote *La Terreur Prussienne,* warning France about Prussia. (Prussia, in 1866, had grabbed Austrian land from Empress Maria Theresa.) To escape swindlers and friends stealing from him, he visited Prague, Budapest, and Vienna, where he was a guest of Emperor Franz Joseph. Dumas wrote to the Goncourt brothers, who reported, "... his letters overflowing with the good will of a child—sparkling with wit."

At sixty-four, he fell in love with an American Jewish girl from New Orleans, Ada Menken, who was young enough to be his granddaughter. She wrote poetry and rode a horse bareback on stage. His son and daughter were horrified. Ada didn't last long, however. She had miles to go and engagements to keep. Oh well—he was happy, despite being penniless again. Michelet, the French historian, told him, "... with my mind I visualize your fights of all kinds. I am so impressed by your indomitable talent which bends and bends again before so many absurd obstacles and not less by your heroic perseverance."

To escape Paris, he went to Roscoff in Brittany to write *Le Grand Dictionaire de Cuisine,* 1,100 pages devoted to mustard, geography, history, and science. To earn money, he toured and lectured to huge audiences. News of the French surrender to the Prussians at Sedan reached him in Marseille and caused him to suffer a slight stroke. He managed to arrive in Paris by train, where his daughter met him and brought him to Brittany, Alexandre *fils* [79] summer home. [80] Dumas told his son about a dream he had—he was standing on the peak of a pyramid on a mountain made up of

---

[79] Puys near Dieppe.

[80] Dumas *fils* was now the famous author of *The Lady of the Camillias,* which was made into a play and then an opera by Verdi (*La Traviata*). He referred to his father as "a child I had when I was very young." He attributed the defeat of France, the Bloody Commune, and the loss of the provinces of Alsace and Lorraine to the Beast of Prostitution, which, by undermining morality, faith, and the family, opened the way to disaster. He wrote, "... the lost creatures who sold pleasure to some and gave it freely to others—who kept for themselves only shame, inevitable ignomiy, and a doubtful future ..."

all his books, piled like blocks of masonry, one on top of the other. Little by little, the ground shifted, slithered, and gave way beneath his feet, and what he had been standing on was nothing but a heap of pumice stones—grey ashes of volcanic lava that had cooled. He asked, "Alexandre, do you think anything of mine will survive?" His son reassured him, "Be at peace. The monument is well built. The base is solid."[81]

Alexandre Dumas *père* died peacefully in his sleep on December 5, 1870, saying of death, "I shall tell her a story, and she will be kind to me." He died surrounded by his family—pampered and loved—never knowing the Prussians were at the gates of Dieppe. The priest of St. Jacques in Dieppe gave him the last rites, and a Mass was held in Neuville near Dieppe. After the war, he was buried in Villers-Cotterêtes beside his parents, who had given birth to a world-renowned genius. Since then, his remains have been transferred to the Panthéon in Paris.

After Dumas' death, Alexandre *fils* wrote to the novelist George Sand (his mother-confessor), "I am reading and rereading him, overwhelmed by his good humor, charm, and power. In his book about Russia in the Caucasus, you travel seven thousand miles without drawing a breath or feeling tired."

VINCENNES

I knew I wanted to go to Vincennes, located on the eastern fringe of Paris, for some reason. I just forgot why. The park in the little residential town is three times larger than Central Park in New York. In the ninth century, French kings hunted wild boar in the forest. Louis VII (Eleanor of Aquitaine's first husband) built a hunting lodge here, and Philip Augustus, married to Anne of Brittany, built a small château. For twenty years, it was the seat of government for King Charles V, who chose the fleur-de-lis as his emblem. King St. Louis IX enlarged the château and held his court under an oak tree. A pyramid marks the spot.

---

[81] Dumas' statue by Gustave Doré in Place Malesherbes was inspired by the dream. Dumas, with a smile, is seated atop a gigantic stone pedestal. At his feet on one side is d'Artagnan, Dumas' favorite character.

After capturing Paris, English King Henry V[82] died at the château in 1422, and Queen Marie de Médici took shelter here after her French husband, Henry IV (who once promised "a chicken in every pot"), was murdered. After Louis XIV moved to Versailles,[83] Louis XVI (who was guillotined) used Vincennes as a prison. Count Mirabeau, who fought against government despotism and corruption before the Revolution, was imprisoned in Vincennes for forty-two months. Conditions were so appalling, his jailers petitioned for his release. During the Third Empire, Napoleon III hired a landscape architect from Bordeaux, Georges Haussmann, who transformed the forest into another Hyde Park with three small lakes, trees, lawns, paths, roads, and a racetrack. The château was closed for repairs, but we visited the chapel in the courtyard where the jewel-like stained glass windows are more awesome than those in St. Chapelle in Paris.[84] My memory of the beautiful park is a steady stream of sweaty joggers. I thought you were supposed to stroll through a park.

COMPIÈGNE

Compiègne on the Oise River adjoining the forest of Villers, is another lovely medieval town less than an hour train ride from Gare du Nord in Paris. We passed the little village of Bethesy near Compiègne, where, in the Middle Ages, Abbé Fortier was both priest and teacher. In his last sermon when he was ninety, he told his parishioners, "I am going to leave you, my children. God gave you to me stupid and stupid I return you."

Compiègne was a favorite retreat for kings and queens, but not for Marie de Médici. Her son, Louis XIII, influenced by Richelieu, imprisoned her in a château in the forest. After World War I, Germany was forced to sign an armistice here on November 19, 1918. During World War II, when Germany defeated France

---

[82] After winning The Battle of Agincourt, he married Catherine de Valois, daughter of French King Charles VI.

[83] Louis XV gave Mme. Pompadour the whole village of Sèvres, where she established porcelain factories.

[84] Modeled after these windows.

in 1940, Hitler demanded that the surrender be signed in the same place where Germany had been forced to surrender—in a replica of the railroad car outside Compiègne. Today it is the main exhibit of a museum there.

From an outdoor table in front of the most beautiful (in my opinion) Hôtel de Ville in France, we watched three *Picantins* in the belfry strike the hour with their mallets. Dressed in King Francis I uniforms, they represent the common people, called *Picantins* or *Jacquemards*. The equestrian statue of Joan of Arc in the large town square, aflame with flowers, commemorates her capture by the Burgundians at Compiègne on May 23, 1430. The day she was taken prisoner with her brother, she had attended Mass at the Church of St. Jacques. Since then, for generations, this church has been a principal place of worship.

At the castle, teenage Marie Antoinette met her future husband before he became King Louis XVI. Our enthusiastic lady guide chuckled a lot in French as she led her troops through a secret door in Napoleon's library, the place where he met his second wife, fourteen-year-old Marie Louise of Austria. After gulping down his dinner, he seduced her. He never did enjoy eating.

Napoleon III and Empress Eugénie invited guests for parties and balls that lasted ten days. It was fun to imagine the American lady visitor who wrote to a friend saying she had to have about twenty dresses for an eight-day visit—a traveling suit, a green dress for the hunt, seven ball dresses, and five gowns for teas. "We followed the lackey's plump, white calves through the long corridors, arriving at last in the salon. All the guests marched in procession through the long gallery, trying not to slip on the waxed floor. One hundred people were seated at the table. I never saw such a tremendous long stretch of white linen."

During the French Revolution, sixteen Carmelite nuns were arrested and taken in open carts to Paris where they were executed for "harboring arms." As they mounted the scaffold, they sang *Salve Regina* and chanted *Laudate Dominum*. Francis Poulenc immortalized them in his opera *Les Dialogues des Carmelites*.

Portraits of dresses worn at Eugénie's court reminded me of one man's observation: "Women heave, groan, belch, and squirm. Bosoms pop out of the top of dresses like champagne corks." During the Franco-Prussian War in 1870, Empress Eugénie fled to England. The composer Bizet and his wife, Genevieve, fled to Compiègne, where he wrote, "Here we are, deep in Germany with 4,000 Prussians stationed at Compiègne." After inspecting tapestries, furniture, and paintings, on the way back to the train it was a relief to return to reality. Two little boys from a third-story window were relieving themselves on people passing by.

TROYES
King Arthur's Court—Crown of Thorns

The picturesque capital of the Champagne region is forty-five minutes from the Paris railroad station Gare de l'Est. We headed for Old Town through flower-filled squares and parks. In the twelfth century, Eleanor of Aquitaine's daughter, Marie, wife of the count of Champagne, commissioned Crétien de Troyes to write, for the first time, stories of King Arthur's court. In his wildly imaginative *The Grail*, the hero, Perceval, follows his mother's advice and gives comfort to every disconsolate maiden he sees.

Troyes is a delightful surprise with one medieval house after another and beautiful twelfth-century churches—nine of them. St. Madelèine's, with its spectacular rood screen, is the oldest. In St. Urban's Basilica, a statue of a young, amused Madonna holds her chubby infant clutching a bunch of grapes. St. Nizier's is named for a seventh-century bishop of Bescançon, a friend of Pope Gregory the Great.[85] The amazing rose window in the Cathedral of St. Peter and St. Paul is modern, and the stained glass windows are as dazzling as those in St. Chapelle in Paris.

At Troyes, King St. Louis IX came from Paris to meet Venetian representatives who were bringing him Jesus' Crown of Thorns, which the king had purchased.[86] After receiving the precious relic,

---

[85] Responsible for the conversion of England and the Gregorian Chant.

[86] The Venetians and their allies, the Fourth Crusaders, had sacked Christian Byzantine Constantinople and divided the loot.

King Louis walked barefoot in procession from Troyes to Vincennes, holding Christ's Crown of Thorns above his head. Then he continued walking to Nôtre Dame in Paris.[87] When his arms became tired, Dominican priests helped prop them up.

The cathedral in Troyes was consecrated in 1430, a year after Joan of Arc and the newly-crowned Dauphin passed through the city. Ten years before (while the king was recovering from a bout of insanity), the Dauphin's promiscuous mother had signed a treaty at Troyes giving both the throne of France and her daughter, Catherine, to English King Henry V. Their wedding took place in the Church of St. Jean in St. Jean's Square, where medieval fairs were held. Like the Canal de la Haute Seine flowing through Troyes, the city today is serene and leisurely. Definitely a "go-back-to" town.

AMBOISE
Leonardo Da Vinci

At Amboise (on the Loire River), where Charles VIII banged his head on a door and died, we toured the beautiful castle on a hill. During the season, buses from every tour company in Europe are here. We escaped most of the tourists, but not the flocks of school children. The main attraction is the home of Leonardo da Vinci—the engineer, scientist, architect, musician, and philosopher from Vinci, Italy. He said, "He who does not punish evil, commands it to be done," and, "Just as iron rusts from disuse, even so does inaction spoil the intellect."

In 1516, French King Francis I, who lived in Amboise, invited the genius to come to France. At sixty-three, white-bearded da Vinci accepted the invitation, packed *Mona Lisa*,[88] *John the Baptist*, and *The Virgin and Child Jesus with St. Anne* in leather saddle bags, and, with two companions, crossed the Italian Alps on a mule.

---

[87] He built Sainte Chapelle in the 13th Century to house the relics. They are now in the cathedral treasury of Nôtre Dame de Paris.

[88] He worked on the portrait so long (four years), Mona Lisa's husband refused to pay for it. King Francis I bought it for $50,000. While painting *The Last Supper*, he had trouble finding the right model for Judas' face. He said he might have to use the face of the prior of the church (who was bugging him to finish). That ended the harassment.

Finally, peace and quiet after a lifetime of wars and political turmoil. Although a stroke had affected his right arm and he could no longer paint, he continued researching and worked on hydraulic inventions for flood control. He died on May 2, 1519.

A tour of his small, elegant home, *Le Close Luce*,[89] begins in a long gallery where the king and his friends sat to enjoy da Vinci's elaborate spectacles lit by four hundred double candelabras. The last room on the tour is a display of more than forty fantastic machines built by IBM, that represent da Vinci's inventions. Bored, nonscientific women glanced at the complicated machines and waited impatiently for husbands and teenagers who found the exhibit "awesome."

The tour ended in a garden where roses bloomed. Along one side of the garden, you can buy ice cream cones or soft drinks and sit at tables. A video presentation upstairs over the souvenir shop explains that when da Vinci lived here, a large park separated *Le Close Luce* from the castle. An underground passage connected his home to the castle. Today the short distance is covered by streets, shops, and restaurants.

ANGERS,[90] ROCHEMENIER AND CLÉRY
English King Henry II, Troglodite Caves, Spider King (Louis XI)

At Angers, capital of the former province of Anjou, a beautiful thirteenth-century castle on a hill overlooks the Maine River and the countryside. King Saint Louis IX rebuilt the château into a fortress modeled after those built by Crusaders in Jerusalem. We entered on a drawbridge over a moat. In the chapel, we happened upon a concert of incredibly ethereal, difficult, medieval music. Good King René, count of Anjou and patron of arts, designed the gorgeous rose gardens. His interest in horticulture has been carried on through the centuries: Angers has a worldwide reputation for its university specializing in horticulture.

The castle belonged to the counts of Anjou. Unfortunately, the first count was related to William the Conqueror, who conquered

---

[89] Virgin of Light.
[90] *Angers* means "black," named for the slate quarries.

England in 1066. His descendant[91] had a son (King Henry II) who inherited his father's lands in Normandy. When he married Eleanor of Aquitaine, he also inherited her lands, embroiling Anjou and England in a three-hundred-year war. His kingdom stretched from northern England down to the Pyrenees.

During World War II, the castle of Angers was used by the Germans to store ammunition. The RAF[92] bombed it, but the Cathedral of St. Maurice was left intact. The cathedral has a stained glass window depicting the life of Thomas à Becket, Archbishop of Canterbury, who defied his old friend King Henry II and was murdered. We stayed at Hôtel Le Progrés, and ate kangaroo and *champagne chaude* (potato and ham salad) at a restaurant called La Carnivores. The main reason for going to Angers, however, was to rent a car[93] and visit a troglodyte village at Rochemenier near Samur, where people lived in caves until 1930. We saw ovens carved into the limestone rock. Some caves are still used as wine or mushroom cellars. During World War II, the stained glass windows of the cathedral were stored in the caves.

Then on to the Basilica Nôtre Dame de Cléry (ten miles from Orléans), where my favorite French king, Louis XI (the "Spider King),"[94] is buried. Also buried in the Basilica is Joan of Arc's "Gentle Bastard," Dunois.[95] Both Joan of Arc and the Spider King had a special devotion to Our Lady of Cléry.

The original statue that the Spider King designed for himself shows him in a kneeling position, hands clasped in prayer, dressed as a hunter. The statue, destroyed by the Huguenots in 1562, was restored by King Louis XIII (the one domineered by Cardinal Richelieu). The sculptor, Boudin, captures the Spider's piety in the same kneeling position, but now he is clothed in a flowing court robe. Gone, too,

---

[91] Geoffrey IV. His wife was related to William the Conqueror, the first Norman king of England. (His real name was William II, Duke of Normandy.)

[92] Royal Air Force.

[93] Ibiza Essence.

[94] The Spider King was the son of King Charles VII, the one Joan of Arc practically hauled to Reims to be crowned king of France

[95] Dunois was the Dauphin's relative, head of Orléans's defense.

is the Spider's favorite dog, replaced by four chubby cherubs—one on each corner of the tomb. We climbed a beautiful spiral staircase to see a little cubbyhole where the king could peek down during Mass without being seen. As a thank you for the visit to Our Lady of Cléry,[96] we were treated to a brilliant full-size rainbow.

Although it was dark when we returned to Angers, we found another favorite chapel of the Spider King—Béhuard—outside town, on an island in the Loire. As a teenager, the king had been miraculously saved from drowning and gave all the credit to the Blessed Mother for answering his desperate prayers. Safe on land, he walked to the nearby ancient chapel of Our Lady of Béhuard to thank her. Her statue and chapel are on top of a small rocky cliff. Alone in the dark quiet night, we visited the Spider King's Virgin holding her Infant.

---

[96] In 1280, when a statue was found in the village, Cléry became a place of pilgrimage. When Spider defeated the English against great odds at Dieppe as a teenage commander, he went to Cléry to thank the Virgin. He had promised her, if victorious, to enlarge and glorify her church.

4

LA VENDÉE

CHOLET

A FRIEND FROM the Vendée told us where to visit in the Vendée region (near La Rochelle). This region extends ninety-three miles along the Atlantic, from the Loire to the Gironde estuaries. During the French Revolution, the residents of the Vendée region—a peaceful people—attempted to defend their persecuted clergy, resist higher taxes, and refuse forced conscription into the republican army. One hundred fifty thousand people, including women and children, were massacred by the revolutionary armies. Priests and nuns were drowned and thrown to angry mobs. Near Cholet at the Grand Parc du Puy (the first historic and ecological park in Europe), a spectacular outdoor evening extravaganza, *Puy du Fou*, commemorates the history of the Vendéans from the Middle Ages.

During the day, we wandered around a reconstructed medieval village where costumed craftsmen, musicians, and falconers entertained the crowds. It rained off and on, but that was okay—we had raincoats and umbrellas. During the worst downpour, we took shelter in a covered picnic area, pulled out our ever-ready wine bottle, along with bread, cheese, and mustard, and watched good-natured, soaking-wet people of all ages. The weather cleared in time for an outdoor dinner with waitresses and musicians dressed in regional costumes. We sat with two delightful young couples from Dijon who had recently moved to Paris. We hurried through dessert and dashed with other tourists to catch *le petite train,* waiting to take us to the amphitheater to see the greatest sound and light show in France, *Puy du Fou.*

The stage area covers thirty-two acres, including a lake and a sixteenth-century château silhouetted against the evening sky. A bright sliver of the moon was a bonus. Translation headphones are provided for English, Japanese, and German visitors. Each group is assigned to a certain area in the 12,500 seat stadium. The famous spectacle, started in 1978, involves 650 people and fifty horsemen, and is narrated by actors from the *Théâtre Molière* and the *Comédie Française.* The drama begins in the twelve hundreds and highlights the experiences of a noble family through five generations.

An explosion of 1,500 lights transplanted us from darkness to a day in the thirteenth century. Horsemen gallop along the shore of the lake in front of the medieval château, protecting it, while in the fields, peasants harvest wheat. Later, villagers in Renaissance finery pay homage to King Francis I. Centuries come and go until 1793, when revolutionary troops in red and blue uniforms burst on the scene, scattering and killing peasants and nobles alike. Cannons roar, and a blazing castle burns before our eyes with a riotous display of fireworks in the dark sky. The two-hour history ends like a happily-ever-after story, depicting an era of peace with 1,480 fountains as a backdrop for aquatic ballerinas.

LES SABLES D'OLONNE

The next day we drove about an hour, from Chôlet in the Vendée to Les Sables (Sand) d'Olonne, my friend Danniell's hometown. It is only a dot on the map, but the beach that stretches forever was strewn with hundreds of sunbathing bodies. There are three ports: fishing, commerce, and pleasure. The nonstop around-the-world sailing regatta, "The Vendée Globe," begins and ends in Les Sables-d'Olonne.

We drove around in circles in the beach area looking for the tourist office, but had to give up. We settled for a drink on the Thaloussa Hotel veranda, overlooking the ocean and bay where people were taking sailing lessons. A physical therapist had told us the hotel is famous for seaweed massages. Instead of basking in the sun, we should have been wallowing in seaweed.

We had promised my friend we would get acquainted with her country. Every time we saw a town or church, we stopped. As we drove through the flat, western terrain, we remembered the thousands of people who had been driven from their homes by the revolutionists during the Vendéan rebellion in the 1790s. The women were as brave as those in the French Resistance during World War II. One woman wrote, "I saw forty-two of my relatives perish, but the murder of my father before my very eyes filled me with such rage, I resolved to sacrifice my body to the king and offer my soul to God. I swore to fight until death or victory."

Another woman was imprisoned despite the fact that her husband, a general in the Vendéan war, had saved five thousand republican soldiers. All appeals to authorities had failed. In a last attempt, she sent her four-year-old daughter to the officer-in-charge, requesting a letter of pardon for the little girl's father. The officer must have had a daughter of his own. He told the little girl to sing a song. What she sang was, "Long live the king and down with the Republic." Fortunately, he laughed. After a few derogatory remarks about fanatical Royalists, he gave her the letters of pardon, which she carried triumphantly back to Mama.

We drove through La Roche-sur-Yon, a railroad town, which was the chief town of the Vendée under Napoleon. Then on to Fontenay-le-Comte, which is one of the most picturesque towns in France. In all the churches, stained glass windows depict the martyrdom of parishioners.

At St. Hilaire de Talmont, the medieval church is named for a fourth-century bishop of Poitiers, but it is their native son, St. Henri Dorie (1839–1866) they honor. At eighteen, with ten other missionaries, he left Marseille for Korea via Ceylon, Singapore, Cambodia, Saigon, and

Hong Kong. In Korea, near Seoul, he cared for the poor and preached the gospel. Eight months later, along with three other priests, he was tortured and beheaded.

LUÇON

The bishopric of Luçon belonged to Cardinal Richelieu (1585–1642). His brother, who wanted to be a monk, was supposed to have inherited it, but he wasn't twenty-five, the required age. Richelieu lied to Pope Paul V and substituted his own name for his brother's. Opposite the church is a statute of Richelieu, who managed to manipulate King Louis XIII throughout his life.

ST. LAURENT-SUR-SÈVRE
St. Louis de Montfort (1673–1716)

The lovely, peaceful town is a pilgrimage center enclosed within miles of walls. St. Louis Marie de Montfort (1673–1716) is buried here. Like St. Francis of Assisi, he was another holy oddity. Born in the small town of Montfort near Rennes in Brittany, he left home at nineteen, after studying for the priesthood for eight years, and set out for St. Sulpice Seminary in Paris. He gave all his money and baggage to the first beggar he met, and even exchanged clothes. Begging food and shelter along the way, he walked 163 miles to Paris, in total surrender to God to take care of him. At St. Sulpice, he studied eight more years, and on June 5, 1700, celebrated his first Mass at the Altar of Our Lady. In Poitiers, he preached devotion to Mary and Jesus and cared for the poor in a filthy, dark, poorhouse asylum. With him were five or six brothers and a nun, Marie Louise Trichet, who founded the charitable order Daughters of Wisdom.

Not sure of his role—maybe he should be a hermit, or a foreign missionary—he walked to Rome, where Pope Clement XI told him to continue his work. Because of his undignified, vagabond lifestyle, several bishops exiled him. He was so poor, even the poor took up a collection to buy him warm clothes. In Pontchâteau, he erected a life-size Calvary on a hill with his followers, but the bishop, with orders from Paris, refused to bless it. He was told (after a year's work) to tear it down because it might be used to signal the enemy, the British. He was even poisoned. His health deteriorated and he collapsed while preaching a mission at St. Laurent-sur-Sèvre, and died in 1716 at forty-three. He is buried at St. Laurent in a chapel at the top of a hill. Along each side of a staircase leading up to the chapel are sculpted angels with enormous wings. Today, Montfort missionaries dedicated to the Blessed Virgin and the Holy Spirit are worldwide.

LA ROCHELLE

Someday I'll go to La Rochelle in the off-season to see the old girl in her everyday clothes. In August, she's dressed to show off. The sun shines and the water in the harbor sparkles for crowds of people in front-row seats at sidewalk cafés. Medieval towers, bobbing yachts, and sailboats are picture-perfect.

Old Town is an architectural gem with Roman, Gothic, and Renaissance churches and buildings that feature arcades, wrought-iron balconies, and half-timbered houses. Everywhere, gargoyles, lions, and dolphins peer down from windows and doors. On rue du Palais, we searched for and found a covered passageway that led to a courtyard (once the site of a Knight Templar Commanderie) where an enormous Maltese Cross is emblazoned on the pavement. Their commander's tomb is beneath a restaurant on the square, and at certain hours you can visit. The tourist office has free yellow bicycles for rides along the harbor or through the enormous park. We also found two perfect restaurants, Art Nouveau Café de Paris on rue Verdun, and, near the harbor, Comédie Français, decorated with posters, theatre decor, and stage props. My favorite was a curly-headed little clown wearing clamshell shoes and playing a fiddle.

Old Town, loaded with local color, bustled with entertainment. In the busy marketplace, a man and his eleven-year-old son were making caramelized candy. In one square, an audience watched a big man riding a tiny bicycle and a cat tiptoeing on top of milk bottles. Around the corner, a crowd gathered to hear South American musicians from Peru. At night, romantically lit buildings, especially Diane de Poitiers' courtyard, created beauty and mystery. She was King Henri III's mistress—twenty years older than he. She wrote, "The years that a woman deducts from her age are never lost. They are added on to another woman."

We had planned to take a long excursion boat ride, but reservations are necessary the day before. We settled for a forty-five minute ride around the harbor. In the twelfth century, during Eleanor of Aquitaine's time, wine and salt were stashed on vessels sailing to England and the Netherlands. From the fourteenth to the sixteenth century, La Rochelle was one of France's great maritime cities—furs arrived from Canada, and sugar, slaves, and indigo from Santo Domingo—but Louis XV put a stop to all that. If you want to know more history, you'll have to buy the video *The Three Musketeers*. The old version is hysterical.

The most unexpected surprise was Alain Quemper's multimedia film at the Maritime Museum, entitled *Words of the Fisherman* and based on the novel *Pêcheur d'Islande*, or *Iceland Fisherman*, by the genius writer Pierre Loti. The twenty-five-year project honors generations of professional fishermen whose livelihood depended on cod from the dangerous, rocky coast of Iceland, 1,400 miles away. Each year in February, French vessels with crews of six left from Normandy, Boulogne, and Dunkirk, returning on the first of August to escape the fog that lasts sometimes as long as ten days—so heavy the men couldn't see each other.

The film captures low-hanging clouds, the pale silver-rose nightless summers, and close-up faces of men who risked their lives fighting the monumental forces of nature. We see them first in home-knit blue wool sweaters and tar-soaked cloth caps, preparing hooks and lines. Later we see them in oilskins "glossy as shark skins," collars pulled tightly around their necks with tarred cord, which also binds their wrists and ankles. We see them with ice-covered beards battling fierce waves waiting to devour them. We hear the roar of water crashing on deck, ready to smash them to pieces—"waves like a mountain range with ever-deepening alleys."

All day at the helm, a man shivers from the cold—hands numb. Others hold the same positions all day, their reels and rods drilled into holes, faces and eyes exposed to blinding snow and hail—fearless men with complete confidence in themselves, their vessel, and their faith in the Virgin, "Star of the Sea."

On shore, women wait for husbands, lovers, and sons. Maybe two boats arrive in August. Three days later, a few more vessels appear on the horizon. A week passes. As many as twelve arrive. Weeks drag on. A few women continue to hope, waiting for ships that never return.

Directed by Jean-Marie Sittler, the film is a denunciation of the political and economic establishment that has extinguished a way of life. No longer can a man choose his destiny. "Tomorrow must change this," is the Iceland fishermen's vow, *Paroles de Marin* (*Words of the Fishermen*).

HONFLEUR
Samuel de Champlain (1567–1635)

The port of Honfleur in Normandy is every visitor's happy memory, with its harbor, yachts, fishing boats, and cafés. Across the street from our hotel, Cheval Blanc, overlooking the harbor, we danced in the street to the music of a French band playing American country rock songs.[97] Amber lights sparkling on the water cast a dreamy spell over everyone except the busy waiters.

Once, the quay was teeming with raucous, weather-beaten seamen, merchants, and prostitutes. The harbor was crowded with cod and whaling ships. During the reign of French King Henri IV (1553–1610), one ship captain was Samuel de Champlain, who may have been one of King Henri IV's eleven[98] illegitimate children. He wrote, "His majesty to whom I was bound by birth, as by the pension with which he honored me." There is no record of his birth or baptism. He was brought up in Brouage in the Basque Country, as the son of a seaman who instructed young Samuel in navigation as a child. As a teenager, the boy sailed with his uncle to the West Indies, the Canary Islands, and South America on Dutch, Portuguese, and Basque ships.

During the horrible religious wars in Europe, although he fought under Huguenot Henri of Navarre (who later became King Henri IV),

---

[97] Lynyrd Skynyrd and Dave Matthews Band.
[98] At least.

Champlain always dreamed of a new and better land where men could live in peace and charity. Seventeen years before the Puritans landed at Plymouth Rock in 1603, he was ordered to accompany an Atlantic expedition as an observer and report directly to the king. He sketched maps from Hudson Bay down to the Great Lakes on pieces of white birch bark, and wrote three books.[99]

Champlain in an Indian Canoe, 1603

The next year he explored as far as Cape Cod, and founded another colony, Acadia.[100] As the king's servant, he was ordered to provide a base for exploring and trading in furs and codfish. He left from Honfleur in 1608, sailed up the St. Lawrence River, and founded Quebec, which the Indians called *Kwebec* (an Algonquin word for "narrowing of the river"). From there, he discovered Lake Champlain and befriended the Huron Indians. Of all the explorers, only Champlain had good

---

[99] The three books are *Voyages de la Nouvelle, France* and *Traitte de la Marine, et du Devoir d'um.*

[100] Acadia today is part of Nova Scotia and Brunswick in Canada.

rapport with the Indians. He treated them with respect, admired their good qualities, and was able to prevent many uprisings before they happened. When he invited different tribes to Quebec, after a week of feasting and wild, ritual dancing, the Algonquians brought him to Ticonderoga, a name that meant "Two large beautiful lakes." These came to be known as Lake George and Lake Champlain.

After one voyage, he presented the king with five young geese that ended up in the pools at Fontainebleau. Another time, he returned with a reindeer and a moose as big as a horse for the king's four-year-old son, the future King Louis XIII. Once, he brought back an Indian who paddled a red canoe with incredible speed down the Seine in front of the Louvre.

From Honfleur, Champlain practically commuted to the New World. He crossed the Atlantic twenty-seven times without losing a ship. Through negotiations, he tried to keep peace with the Indians who were constantly at war with each other. "They have spoken to me about it many times and have often asked my advice which was that they should make peace with one another, and we would assist them." But, as Shakespeare's Hamlet said, "Ah, there's the rub."[101] By helping one tribe, he made enemies of others.

The early camaraderie with the Hurons didn't last. In a war[102] during which he helped two Iroquois tribes[103] defeat the Hurons,[104] two arrows pierced his leg and knee. He was strapped into a basket and carried on the backs of strong Indians who took turns carrying him and the wounded seventy-five miles through snow, hail, and heavy winds to their hidden canoes. Champlain wrote that the pain of being bound was worse than his wounds.

For twenty-two years, Champlain struggled to keep his colonies intact despite enemies who appeared at the French court after King Henri IV was assassinated. Each time he returned from France, his settlements were in ruins and his people were starving: "We were eating our peas very sparingly." In his reports to the king and in books about the Indians, he wrote that there was no law among them. The only rule they knew was retaliation and sadistic torture. The chief had no authority. The Indians

---

[101] Shakespeare's *Hamlet* Act III, scene 1, lines 65–68.

[102] Past Lake Ontario ten miles south of Conestoga, New York.

[103] The Oneida and Anandoga.

[104] Another Iroquois tribe that had attacked them.

acted for themselves. Indian women sampled twenty or more men before choosing one. One night the fleas in his bed were so bad, he slept outdoors on the ground. In the dark, a squaw "offered herself" to him. He wrote, "I declined with thanks and returned to the fleas." He also wrote, "An Indian girl keeps company with whomever she likes. By that method, she selects a partner who pleases her most for her husband. They live together for the rest of their lives." No wonder Champlain was anxious to bring missionaries to civilize them. The Jesuits even formed an Indian boys' choir and taught them to sing the "Our Father" in their native language.

In 1610, at the age of forty, he married twelve-year-old Hélène Boullé, whose wealthy father was a powerful comptroller at the French court. They were married in Paris at Église St. Germaine l'Auxerrois. When his bride ran away, her parents tracked her down and made her return to her husband. In 1620, at the age of twenty-two, she sailed with him from France on a terrifying storm-tossed voyage, and stayed in the freezing cold wilderness for five years. She studied the Algonquin language, cared for the Indian women and children, and talked to them about Christ and her Christian faith. She also managed Champlain's investments in commercial companies.[105] When Quebec and Acadia were seized by the British in 1629, Champlain was taken to London as a prisoner. Three months before the surrender, a Peace Treaty had been signed, but it was illegal. Champlain worked for three years to regain his settlements.[106] After thirty years of struggle and frustration, he had a stroke. Paralyzed for over two months, he died in the wilderness, a convert to Catholicism. His beautiful city, Quebec, Canada, with its quaint, cobblestone buildings and straggly streets with French names, is far from Honfleur, but it is Champlain's dream come true, especially at Christmas, the anniversary of the day he died.

Erik Satie (1866–1925) Writer, Composer, Pianist

"If I have to follow someone,
I think I can say it's just going to be me."

---

[105] After Champlain's death, she became an Ursuline nun.
[106] Quebec was formally returned in 1633 by the Treaty of Saint Germain en Laye.

A friend who had wandered off to explore Honfleur came rushing back to our hotel to tell us about a wonderful museum she had discovered, Erik Satie's birthplace. The next day, we found the museum at 9 rue Haute, on a street that once was lined with homes of wealthy merchants and civic leaders. What a fun museum! We especially enjoyed Satie's recorded ragtime music and the big circus carousel there reminiscent of the ballet *Parade* about circus performers for which he composed the score.

> As for me, I was born in Honfleur (Calvados) in the Pont l'Eveque district on May 17, 1866 ... Honfleur is a small town watered by the poetic waves of the Seine ... Its inhabitants are very polite and very agreeable ...
>
> —ERIK SATIE

He also wrote, "Following a rather short adolescence, I became an ordinary young man; tolerable but no more. At that moment in my life, I began to think and write. Oh yes, wretched idea ... very wretched idea!"[107]

And that's the way it was—a long, lonesome journey: "What did I come to do upon this earthly, earthy earth? Thinking it was the right thing to do—almost as soon as I arrived down here—I started playing snatches of music which I made up myself ... All my troubles stem from this ...."

Trouble, yes, but he was blessed with a sense of humor and wild imagination: "Before writing a work, I walk around it several times accompanied by myself."[108] His memory of studying at the Paris Conservatory was a nightmare. After a sadistic teacher informed him he was worthless and insignificant, he enlisted in the Infantry. To be discharged, he deliberately ran miles and miles cross-country in the cold to get sick—which he did. He had bronchitis for three months.

In Paris, when Satie was twenty-one, the poet Contamine de Latour got him a job as a pianist playing music-hall tunes at *Le Chat Noir*, an "artistic" cabaret on Montmartre. The cabaret is gone, but not Steinlen's painting of a black cat, the cafe's symbol. Shy and conservative, Satie grew a beard, let

---

[107] From "Hidden Corners of My Life."
[108] From a piano duet, "Unpleasant Glimpses," 1912.

his hair grow, and became one of the starving Bohemians on Montmartre. His only love affair was with promiscuous Suzanne Valadon, mother of Maurice Utrillo. "Love is a sickness of the nerves. It's serious, yes, very serious ... Myself, I'm afraid of it. I avoid it." After she left him, he started a church.[109] He preached and wrote articles deploring the loss of religion. "We can only watch with regret as men offend God every day by their ignorance of the divine precepts of the gospel ... flee from pride. Of all our afflictions, this is the most constipating."

He was so poor, he and his friend Contamine took turns wearing the same suit. "It's odd. You find people in every bar willing to offer you a drink. No one ever dreams of presenting you with a sandwich." Excited by exotic music he heard from other countries at the 1889 Paris Exposition, he composed innovative tunes and rhythms[110] that traditionalists ridiculed. "I have against me one thousand unpleasant people." Satie's compositions included instructions for playing. One passage, for example, was to "Make a sound like a nightingale with a toothache."

When his father, a shipbroker and musician, sent him money, he bought a velvet jacket, a monocle, and an umbrella. At forty, after years of contempt from critics, he enrolled in d'Indy's Schola Cantorum. Three years later, he graduated at the head of his class. But suddenly his money was gone. "While I was studying, Crac! Poverty arrived like a sad, little girl with large green eyes." He moved from Montmartre to the suburb Arcueil (22 rue Couchy) where he lived for twenty-seven years, walking back and forth from there to Paris[111] to work at night. In his room over a café, he dreamed and drew sketches of magical houses, manors, and châteaux.

At Arcueil, he gave singing and piano lessons to neighborhood children, composing pieces for their little hands and accompanied by words[112] they could understand and visualize in the music (for example, "Light as an egg"). In one piece, describing the sea, he wrote notes on the staff in wavy lines. "Le Bain de Mer" is one of many pieces he composed to accompany drawings by the artist Charles Martin for a collection called "Sport and Divertissements" (Sports and Amusements).

---

[109] Église Métropolitan d'Art.
[110] His music influenced Ravel, Debussy, Saint-Saens, and other French Composers.
[111] 6 miles.
[112] Words by Contamine.

The sea is wide, Madame
In any case, it is pretty deep.
Do not sit on the bottom.
It is very damp.
They are full of water
You are completely soaked
"Yes, I am, Sir."

"Le Bain de Mer"

Also in the suburb of Arcueil, he organized concerts in the little hall where working-class people could benefit from famous poets, musicians, artists, and actors. He took children on outings, started a youth club for orphans, and published a local newspaper. One ad he wrote for the newspaper was headlined, "Attacked by Hoodlums":

A local young man comes out of it very well inflicting considerable damage on his abominable assailants ... How? Because he assiduously took physical culture courses at the Arcueil-Cachan Youth Club.

In 1914, he attended smoky Communist cell meetings with radical, militant loudmouths, but left them because "Communists are disconcertingly bourgeois in matters of art." He loved the scandal he caused. During World War I, he joined the Home Guard. When cannons thundered over Paris, "I nearly got killed. The shells were terribly close to me. People were killed ... a bit of luck, eh ... At the foot of the obelisk at Place de la Concorde, I had a feeling of being sheltered ..."

In 1917, during the war, he collaborated with twenty-seven-year-old Jean Cocteau,[113] who wrote the scenario for Diaghilev's Ballets Russes production of *Parade*. Picasso designed the costumes, sets, and the circus stage curtain with a horse, a bullfighter, a ladder, a dog, and an angel. The choreographer was Leonide Massine. The theme was a publicity parade in which three groups of circus people try to attract an audience for an indoor performance. To Satie's dismay, Cocteau had added all sorts of sound effects—fog horns, cowbells, train whistles, sirens, even typists clicking away on typewriters. During rehearsal, one indignant, horrified musician in the orchestra shouted at Satie, "You must think I am stupid!" Satie said, "I don't think you are stupid. Then again, I may be wrong." Artists loved it, but a man in the audience said if he had known how absurd it was, he would have brought his children. On opening night, the audience

---

[113] Poet, artist, composer, and film maker who composed the score for *Beauty and the Beast*. Visit his painting in Villefranche-sur-mer in the chapel of Saint-Pierre-des Pecheurs (patron saint of sinners). He considered this the most important work of his life.

rioted, and reviews were scathing. "All my old and new enemies did their best to ruin the performance. *Parade* separated me from a great many friends." (Including Debussy.)

The title, *Parade,* was taken from the dictionary: "A comic act put on outdoors by a traveling theatre group to entice people to come inside to see the show." The ballet depicted three barkers trying to lure an imaginary crowd into a tent by staging samples of what they would enjoy inside—a Chinese conjurer, two acrobats, and a young American girl—but nobody enters. After the last number in *Parade*, the sad, disappointed, exhausted barkers collapse in each other's arms.

The audience liked Picasso's curtain, as light-hearted as a circus poster, but booed the ballet—yelling, hissing, and causing a riot. Cocteau recalled, "The women had their hat pins out and would probably have stabbed us to death if it weren't for the presence of the poet, Apollinaire,[114] who was in uniform with a great bandage around his head from his wound." Cocteau, who was an ambulance driver in the war, wrote, "I am anything but this frozen wreck traveling the roads. I am swallowing my tears."

After 1919, Satie became a celebrity in high society. He also caught the flu during the influenza epidemic that killed over one million people. In the United States alone, a half million died.

Satie called his background music "furniture" music. "It fills the same purpose as light, heat, and all forms of comfort ... We must bring about music that is like furniture. I think of it as melodious—softening the noise of knives and forks." His *Socrate* is a musical recitation dedicated to the Greek philosopher Socrates.[115] Satie and Socrates were kindred spirits. Socrates, at court in Athens, refused to worship the officially-recognized gods of the State, and Satie refused to conform to autocrats who set musical standards. They were both "oddities." To make sure his music in *Socrate* evoked delicate, tranquil beauty, Satie ate only white food.

---

[114] He coined the word *surrealism*— combining the real and unreal—which became a new art movement.

[115] Commissioned by Comtesse de Polignac, one of the heirs of the sewing machine magnate, Isaac Singer, who had twenty-two children by four wives.

When Satie became ill in 1924, Count du Beaumont provided a private hotel room for him. When he had to be hospitalized,[116] Madelèine Milhaud, wife of the composer Daruis Milhaud, packed his bags; Brancusi, the Romanian sculptor, brought him homemade chicken soup and yogurt; and a nurse helped him remember his prayers. "I have great confidence in the good Lord. When I am dead, He will do with me absolutely whatever He likes." Satie died July 1, 1925, on Good Friday, leaving a staggering amount of work. He was buried in the Arcueil cemetery, mourned by all his neighbors. Brancusi sculpted a cross on his tombstone, but only the pedestal remains.

ANGOULÊME AND COGNAC
A Cruise on the Charente River

Angoulême, an old Roman town perched on a balcony with wonderful views, is twenty-three miles from Cognac. The narrow, jagged streets hidden behind buildings reminded me of the nursery rhyme, "There was a crooked man who walked a crooked mile ...." Angoulême hosts an International Comic Festival every January. The French take their comics very seriously. There's even a statue of Hergé, creator of the comic strip *Tintin*, the adventurous little boy. The last duc of Angouleme was King Francis I. Besides bringing Leonardo da Vinci and the sculptor Cellini to France, he fought horrible wars in Italy trying to take Milan. Defeated by Emperor Charles V, he was sent to prison in Madrid in1525, but was freed after a year when he substituted his two little sons, aged eight and seven, to suffer cruel punishment as hostages. His extravagance left France bankrupt. After checking into the Grand Hotel de France with my friend, we met a pretty, twentyish girl who drove us to Jarnac, thirty minutes away.

Jarnac, another old Roman city, is famous for brandy made from white pineau grapes. The wine is distilled twice in copper-pot stills, then aged in oak casks. Eighty percent is exported to Great Britain and the United States. The Dutch called the distilled wine *brande wijn*, or burnt wine. They call the two percent of the brandy that evaporates

---

[116] St. Joseph's Hospital.

"the angels' share." Today the brandy is named Cognac for the city where famous distilleries are located. At Jarnac, we boarded The Royal Cognac barge. As we leisurely cruised down the Charante along the riverbank, we saw the Cognac houses of Hennessy, Courvoisier, Martell, and O'tard. In 1795, Scottish Baron O'tart[117] (called O'tard) bought the castle where French King Francis I was born, knowing that the dungeon walls would provide ideal conditions for aging brandy. Today, O'tard brandy is still aging in the cellars.

After the Civil War in America, all the grapevines in Europe were dying from phylloxera. Thomas Volney Munson, from Denison, Texas, shipped disease-resistant grapevines to Europe to save them. A representative from Cognac, Pierre Viala, spent nearly two years with Munson, loading grapevines onto oxcarts to send down the Red River in Texas, then over to Europe. Between three and four million acres of vineyards were uprooted and replanted with the American root stock. It took over twenty years, but the grapevines in Europe were saved.

One guest aboard the Royal Cognac found a book in the little library about the history of the region. It tells the story of the marriage between the duc of Angoulême and Marie Therese, the daughter of Marie Antoinette and King Louis XVI. She had been a prisoner with her parents in the Temple Tower for three years, but after both parents were beheaded, the seventeen-year-old was released.

If ever there was an ideal way to relax from big-city tension, a cruise aboard the elegant Royal Cognac is the answer. Not a sound—only sparkling bubbles in the water and sensuous, green scenery. On the upper deck in the sunshine, where orange and yellow marigolds in flower boxes nudged red geraniums for more room, we were served breakfast and lunch.

Hâute cuisine on the cruise included local specialties such as *melon au pineau* and *sabayon*, a delicious dessert made with egg whites, sugar and cognac, whisked light as a cloud. One side trip was a visit to the Chez Richon vineyard, where cognac is made. The producers, Francine and Michel Forgeron, have four children who play the piano, saxophone, clarinet, and drums. Daddy Michel plays the trumpet

---

[117] He bought it from Count Jean de Valois from the duchy of Valois in Northern France.

and Mama is the dancer. Beautiful Francine—happy, vivacious, and smart—has the figure of a teenager.

Patrice, captain of the Royal Cognac crew, expertly translated into English Francine's demonstration of how cognac is made. Back aboard our gleaming, white boat, the lazy charm of the Charente River, the delightful crew (three happy girls and Captain Patrice), and our perfect accommodations which included candy and a bouquet of roses, made the Royal Cognac cruise a treasured *souvenir*.

SARLAT
Where a Man Can Get Robbed for a Truffle

Sarlat grew around a twelfth-century monastery. After it decayed, the Cathedral of St. Sacredos was built in the seventeenth century. One of the chapels is now a Museum of Sacred Art, and the former Bishops Palace is a theatre. A twelfth-century domed tower, *Lantern des Morts*, served as a chapel for funerals.

Étienne de La Boétie

Opposite the cathedral is the four-story Renaissance home of Sarlat's sixteenth-century favorite son, poet-lawyer Étienne de La Boétie. At eighteen, he wrote a pamphlet[118] condemning tyranny. He found it unbelievable that people would prefer profit to personal freedom. His belief that Christian charity should include human equality inspired the Huguenots to demand justice and tolerance. His writings influenced Rousseau, the philosopher-writer.[119] When Boétie died at thirty-three, his best friend, the essayist Montaigne,[120] wrote an essay entitled "On Friendship" in memory of Boétie, whose statue stands in the town square.

In 1837, a road[121] was cut through Old Town, where gargoyles hang over the marketplace. Sarlat has great shops and restaurants. We even found a box of Tintin chocolate candy, named for the little boy with the weird hairdo in Hergé's comic strip. Restaurants feature truffle

---

[118] *Servitude Volontaire*.
[119] He wrote the novel *Emile and du Contract Social* in 1762.
[120] 1533–1592.
[121] Called *Traverse*.

sauce,[122] walnut oil for salad dressing, and walnut-flavored liqueur (*Eau de Noix*). In one restaurant, we ate a whole bowl of cherries. "How do I love thee?" Let me count the pits. In a small, shaded square behind England's King Henry II's house, men were playing skittles (nine pins). One street, lined with beautiful, medieval houses, is called rue de Fénelon, named for a family that ruled Sarlat twice.

Francois Fénelon (1651–1715)

The priest-writer was born in Château de Fénelon[123] near Sarlat, and studied for the priesthood at St. Sulpice Seminary in Paris during the reign of King Louis XIV. Everyone was arguing about religion, and the explorer La Salle was claiming Louisiana for France. Fénelon's uncle, the Marquis de Fénelon, introduced him to the Court of Versailles where Mme. de Maintenon befriended him—for a while. He was assigned to educate young girls and King Louis' grandsons. Teaching the seven-year-old dauphin,[124] heir to the throne, was like breaking in a wild stallion. If anything stopped him from having his way—if rain spoiled his plans—he would fly into a rage. Eventually, Fénelon won his love and confidence. His method included exercise, humane discipline, and always trust in God. "Poisonous plays and novels were forbidden." Instead, he taught his pupils to see beauty everywhere—in art, science, and history. He told jokes and wrote character-training stories.

In Fénelon's famous novel *Telemaque*,[125] Ulysses's son Telemachus sails off to find his father who has been missing for twenty years after the fall of Troy. Telemachus is the ideal hero. The moral of the story is that kings exist for the sake of their subjects, not exactly what Louis XIV had in mind. Fénelon's spiritual writings helped countless unhappy people, including Mme. Staël, the most famous female novelist in Europe.[126] She underlined nearly all Fénelon's *Spiritual Counsels*, especially the

---

[122] Truffle slices, shallots, cognac, white wine, and stock.
[123] In Salignac.
[124] duc of Burgundy.
[125] Written in Carennac in the Perigord region.
[126] She was the brilliant daughter of King Louis's finance minister, Jacques Necker.

one that reads: "Eliminate from your daily recreations everything which leads to distractions not necessary to rest your mind ..."

After being promoted to the archbishopric of Cambrai near Lille, Fénelon's former friend, Bishop Bousset (who was jealous and envious of Fénelon's fame and position) betrayed him by condemning his writings. Mme. de Maintenon also betrayed him for political reasons. As archbishop of Cambrai for eighteen years, Fénelon was a model priest. Even duc Henri Saint Simon agreed in his *Memoirs*.

Sarlat is one of the most beautifully restored cities in France, thanks to André Malraux, Minister of Culture Affairs under President de Gaulle. He believed that culture "should cease to be the privilege of people lucky enough to live in Paris or be rich."

André Malraux (1901–1976)

I am an agnostic. I have to be something
For don't forget that I am very intelligent ...
But you know better than I that one cannot escape God ...

His tense, driven face belongs on the prow of a ship plowing through a stormy sea—signifying his life. At twenty-three, with a friend and his wife, Clara, André Malraux went to French Indochina for adventure[127] hacking his way through a steamy jungle to bring back a few artifacts. He was arrested for deporting monuments. After three years, he was finally freed, thanks to his wife, who had rounded up signatures of famous writers who vouched for him. She had not been arrested because "a wife has to follow her husband."

Two years later, Malraux returned to help Vietnamese slave laborers by printing a newspaper in their native language. The paper lasted for twenty-three issues. Communist leader Ho Chi Minh informed him, "If you wish to train intellectuals, go to Moscow. The seed you wish to sow in this country will never sprout."

Back in Paris, he wrote about his trip[128] and became famous. Now that he had money, he wanted to find where the Queen of Sheba's ancestors

---

[127] Cambodia, Laos, Vietnam.
[128] The Conqueror.

once lived. With a friend who owned an airplane, they looked down on a pile of ruins that they decided was the exact location, but they couldn't land because the Bedouins were shooting at them. Returning to Algeria, they were caught in the middle of a cyclone. On Malraux's return, he wrote two more novels,[129] warning the French Protectorate government, "Don't be surprised if the peasants turn Communists."

In 1933, when Hitler seized power in Berlin, Malraux became a Communist "fellow traveler" against the Nazis, but at a writers' conference in Moscow, he accused the Marxists of being opposed to culture, and said Stalin knew less about poetry than metallurgy. When Stalin asked what was new in Paris, Malraux told him, "Laurel and Hardy's movies," and showed him Stan Laurel's famous finger trick. (He also caught Stalin trying to practice it.)

He predicted the Civil War in Spain. General Franco had made too many contradictory promises to the landlords and peasants. During the war,[130] Malraux commanded the Republican International Air Force Squadron—thirty-six daredevils—against the Nazis and Mussolini's Fascists. His crew, which included Communists and mercenaries, never had more than six planes in the air at once, and never more than nine in working order. He bought a few planes from the flea market in Paris, but the bombs had to be thrown out the windows. Malraux commanded his little squadron for seven months until Stalin sent two hundred thousand troops, along with planes and supplies, to form the International Brigade.

When Hitler conquered Paris in 1940, Malraux joined the French Army's Tank Corps, but the tanks weren't fit to be taken outside the training ground. He was taken prisoner near Sens, sixty miles southeast of Paris. His brother Roland, a Resistance leader, helped him escape. "If you shoot Malraux, we'll shoot forty-eight Germans." After paying four million francs and handing over a list of German prisoners, Malraux was free, but the Nazis killed both his brothers.

In 1939, after British Prime Minister Neville Chamberlain signed an appeasement treaty with Hitler, French Général Pétain, a Nazi sympathizer, set up a pro-Nazi government in Vichy, France. Malraux went to Southern

---

[129] *Man's Fate* and *Man's Hope*.
[130] 1936–1939.

France, south of Nazi-occupied Vichy, to join the Resistance underground (the *Maquis*). He invented a uniform, gave himself the title "Colonel Berger," and set up an Inter-Allied Command Post[131] to coordinate the complex Resistance web of fifteen thousand people; most from the Alsace-Lorraine region, where thousands were being sent to concentration camps. With twenty-four others, he arranged the largest parachute drop of the war. Two hundred B-17 bombers ("Flying Fortresses") from America and six Spitfires from England dropped arms and supplies. Women spread out bed sheets as huge, white markers, and farmers and tradesmen brought every cart and vehicle available to collect the containers.

After D-Day in Normandy (June 6, 1944), he was shot during an inspection tour[132] by fleeing Germans, and was taken, unconscious, in an ambulance through Figeac, Albi, and Revel to Toulouse, where he was imprisoned for three weeks. "All night German troops passed by. One morning I heard women's voices shouting the Marseillais. The Germans were gone, and the women had found keys to the cells." Malraux wrote that he was the only one in uniform, which gave him "bizarre authority." With three other officers, he assembled some 1,200 ragged, tortured prisoners who then marched 636 miles from Toulouse to help liberate Lorraine in the Vosges Mountains (between Alsace and Lorraine) and defend Strasboug[133] in the Vercors (a plateau surrounded by mountains of rock). For four months the *Maquis* Resistance fighters had been harassing Nazis troops and tanks. After D-Day, twenty-four thousand Resistance fighters were killed by the Nazis.

> We are alone and haven't received any help
> since the beginning of the battle ...

—HERVIEUX
Military commander of the Vercors Resistance Operation[134]

---

[131] Malraux wrote one of the most famous speeches in French history, honoring Jean Moulin, who unified the French Resistance. Moulin was betrayed and tortured to death.

[132] In Gramat.

[133] In the Cathedral of Nôtre Dame carved on a pink pillar, "In memory of the American officers, non-commissioned officers, and enlisted men who gave their lives to free Alsace 1944–45."

[134] Real name François Huet.

With twenty-two officers from Annecy and the Lorraine Brigade, Malraux fought in below-freezing temperatures until the Allies arrived. In the midst of the bombing, killing, and maimed bodies, one of the chaplains[135] (who was killed) told Malraux that after fifteen years of hearing confessions, he was convinced there was no such thing as a grown-up person. As the song goes, "When will they ever learn?"

Paris was liberated on August 25, 1944. At the bar of the Ritz Hotel, Malraux introduced himself to the famous American writer Ernest Hemingway, who had also fought in Spain. Malraux talked on and on and on, and Hemingway couldn't get a word in edgewise. One of Hemingway's "worthless characters" asked "Papa" (Hemingway) if he could shoot him.

After Germany's surrender, Malraux wrote, "I married myself to France." He had seen how the Communists had infiltrated the Resistance with spies, and now they were infiltrating the French government. He broke with the Communists, and at a speech in Strasbourg for the Congress of National Liberation, he began, "Oh my little Stalinist friends, I don't want to talk to you any more than you want to listen to me."

Général de Gaulle was fascinated by the brilliant intellectual who could, and did, talk for hours about archeology, anthropology, history, and politics—besides having contacts with the Communists. When de Gaulle gave up cigarettes, Malraux said, "If he can do it, I can." As Minister of Information, Malraux said, "My chief task was to prevent each party from grabbing all the bedclothes." Before he died at seventy-four, a reporter asked him what he considered the most important event in our time. Malraux replied, "The return of Satan."

PÉRIGUEUX
Capital of the Dordogne Department

Périgueux, another beautiful old city, is thirty-eight miles north of Sarlat. In the huge, curious Cathedral of St. Front, about thirty children with angelic voices were rehearsing songs for their First Communion. To describe French music is impossible. Heavens! I'm starting to

---

[135] Abbé Magnet.

sound like the taxi driver in Paris when he saw all our luggage: "But Madame, it is impossible!"

In the fourth century, St. Front (named for one of the seventy-two disciples)[136] preached here, and a monastery was built over his tomb. Damaged during the Hundred Years' War[137] and the Wars of Religion, the present-day cathedral—half Roman, half Byzantine (topped with bulbous-shaped domes)— was designed by the architect Abadie, who later designed Sacré Coeur Basilica in Paris.

Outside the cathedral in the market square, vendors under blue awnings were selling their wares to people jostling under bright-colored umbrellas during sporadic showers. The square was alive with intriguing smells and joyous colors. Riotous flowers shared stalls with red, green, yellow, and orange fruits and vegetables. Paté and wine merchants dispensed free samples, and a man slicing ham was singing the same song as the children in the church.

Ruins of a Roman amphitheater stand in the middle of the city, and the medieval church of St. Étienne (once the cathedral) now houses the Museum of Sacred Art. In a shady public garden by the Ile River, there is a bust of a twelfth-century troubadour, Bertran de Born, who sang and strummed politically incorrect songs that English King Henry II[138] (who ruled Southwestern France) did not want to hear. When Bertrand encouraged the English king's youngest son to fight against his own father, Dante, in his Inferno, cast Bertrand into Hell. He should have sent the son's mother, Eleanor of Aquitaine, to Hell for turning her four sons against their father.

LA MALENE AND A BOAT RIDE

A boat ride in the canyon on the Tarn River was a priority. Our reservations at Château de la Malene where the ride starts, had not been confirmed. However, the friendly young girl at the desk made six calls, and—bingo!—Aubèrge de la Cascade in St. Chely du Tarn had an

---

[136] Luke 10:1–24.
[137] 1337–1453. Under England for ten years.
[138] 1133–1189. He inherited Normandy, Maine, Touraine, Brittany, and Anjou in France.

opening. It was only a few miles down the road at St. Enimie (sister of seventh-century Dagobert, king of the Franks). She refused to marry any of the suitors her brother, the king, had selected. He finally forced her to become engaged to one, but her whole body broke out in horrible scabs. Hoping the waters at a spa would help, she set out for Bagnols les Bains in the Lot region. On the way, she and her entourage stopped to drink water from a spring, and almost immediately her skin began to heal. She retraced her steps to return to her brother and do as he wished, but each time she reached the gorge of the Tarn River, her affliction returned. When this happened several times, she decided God wanted her to stay there. She founded a small abbey where she lived the rest of her life as abbess.

Our hotel, once a medieval château, was built into the mountainside in a romantic European musical-comedy setting. We made ourselves at home, then drove back to La Malene to hop into a little rowboat that seats six people—including the navigator, who stood in the back and steered us around shoals, rocks, and shallow water so clear we could count the pebbles on the bottom. We floated down the gorge for forty-five minutes in an ethereal wonderland, below white limestone cliffs silhouetted against a bright, blue sky.

ROCAMADOUR
The Black Virgin

The next day we drove through Rodez, Figeac, and Gramont, and arrived at an intersection called La Hospitalier, once the site of the Crusaders' hospital for pilgrims. The Hospitaliers of St. John guided the pilgrims and protected them from robbers. Today the little village has hotels, restaurants, bars, a train station, and a tourist office. From here, the nighttime view of Rocamadour, "the Holy City," is a sparkly Disney fairyland.

The road winds down into the Alzou Valley to the river area, then up to the city atop a steep cliff. Hôtel Ste. Marie, where we stayed in Rocamadour, is carved into the rock halfway up the mountain. Rocamadour has been a pilgrimage destination since 1166, when Benedictine monks found the uncorrupted body of a little man, buried with a dark, wooden statue of the Virgin and her Infant. The hermit's body has been identified as Zacchaeus from St. Luke's gospel— the tax collector—who climbed a tree to get a better look at Jesus; the same Zacchaeus who became a disciple. No one knows how he arrived here. There are a couple of legends, but he probably came after the Crucifixion with other disciples, including Mary Magdalene, when they were set adrift in a boat to perish at sea. Instead, they miraculously landed at Les Saintes Maries de la Mer near Marseille and, like Mary Magdalene, Zacchaeus spent the rest of his life in a cave praying. He is called St. Amador, Lover of Mary. The monks put his body in a sarcophagus, which they set into a niche carved in the cliff. During the next six years, 116 miracles attributed to the Virgin[139] were recorded. The year before Joan of Arc's victory over the English (1429), thousands came to pray for a miracle. For the next two centuries, kings, queens, peasants, and saints came, as well as troubadours who sang the Virgin's praises.

Rocamadour, Place of Pilgrimage

---

[139] Called the Black Virgin from age and soot from candles.

In the chapel of Nôtre Dame, the ancient, dark, wooden statue of the Madonna sits bolt upright, eyes closed. The Infant in her lap is as stiff and rigid as His mother. Votive candles burn along one wall and, hanging high up, are votive offerings: model ships from sailors saved at sea and prisoners' chains and irons. Many, especially those from Holland and Belgium, were sentenced to walk—with iron rings around their necks, arms, or waists—to Rocamadour as a penance. A law in Liége stated that "any person who strikes another without breaking a limb, but leaving marks, will be obliged to make a pilgrimage to Rocamadour on foot."

After visiting the basilica and chapels of Ste. Anne, St. Blaise, and John the Baptist, we mingled in the sunshine with other souvenir-shopping visitors, then descended 216 steps of the Grand Staircase that pilgrims once climbed on their knees. On the lower level, which is the village, an elevator brings you to the "sacred" level and the chapels. A second elevator is available from the sacred level to the top of the cliff, where a fourteenth-century medieval fortress is now used as a residence for priests and monks.

Francis Poulenc (1899–1963), Composer

We returned to the sacred level to tour the Museum of Sacred Art, where an exhibition was dedicated to French composer and pianist Francis Poulenc. The French writer Colette described him as an overgrown schoolboy with a big, doggy face. His hands, "those great bony structures," stretched over an octave and a half. According to his contemporary, Anatole France, "He taught us to laugh at rogues and fools whom we might otherwise be so weak as to hate." Evidently, Poulenc sailed through life with a multitude of friends, achieving one success after another. In 1936, his deeply religious father died, and the following year, a close friend died in a car crash in Hungary. Despondent and overwhelmed with grief, the life of the lapsed Catholic took a sudden turn when he made a penitential pilgrimage to the shrine of the Black Virgin at Rocamadour. He bought a little picture with the text of the *Litanies to the Black Virgin*, and that night began to compose his famous *Les Litanies a la Vierge*

Noire. Poulenc later said he asked the Virgin to intercede for God's pity on our human frailty and "left with a feeling of unbelievable peace."

His *Les Dialogues des Carmelites* commemorates sixteen nuns of the Carmelite Convent at Compiègne who were guillotined during the French Revolution. His *Mass in G* is dedicated to his father, who, with two brothers, founded the chemical company Poulenc Frères, known today as Rhône-Poulenc, manufacturers of pharmaceuticals and textiles. The Museum of Sacred Art was a serendipity, and so was our perfect hotel. The same hard-working, lovely lady who managed the hotel was also in charge of the hotel restaurant. The funniest photo of the whole trip is the one taken with our waiter: by the time he was through with us (and our fractured French) trying to make decisions, he was a wreck—and looked it. As we gaily waved goodbye, he was still mopping his brow.

ISSOIRE
A Wedding

The excuse for this trip was a wedding in Issoire, in the Auvergne region near Clermont-Ferrand. The volcano-peaked region is where Blaise Pascal perfected his barometer and Pope Urban II preached the First Crusade. Through rain and hail, we drove to Issoire. By the time we arrived, we were hungry and had forgotten that the chef doesn't show up until 7:30 p.m. (and no way can you eat until after 8:00 p.m.) Finally, at the appointed hour, we walked into a restaurant with peach-colored tablecloths, silver, and crystal. To our surprise, the headwaiter refused to serve us, despite many tables without "reserved" signs. When we insisted on knowing why, he became unglued! He went berserk, like Mr. Fawlty in *Fawlty Towers*.

The next day at the wedding in twelfth-century St. Austremoine Cathedral, the tiny, brunette bride, Sandrine, in her Paris-creation gown, and the handsome groom, blond Christophe, in a white suit, were united in marriage. After the ceremony, while official papers were being signed on the altar, guests gathered in front of the church, waiting to throw rose petals at the newly married couple. Then it was off to an outdoor reception at twilight in a wooded equestrian area overlooking a tranquil river north of town. From there, to a formal dinner in the countryside south of town. The road into the restaurant's guest parking was blocked by cows returning to the barn for the evening. This was our first French wedding. The reception, consisting of a seven-course dinner with appropriate wines, lasted five hours. Throughout the evening, everyone sang happy, joyous French songs. Dancing began before the dessert and coffee, and lasted all night— or so they told me.

BERGERAC AND EDMOND ROSTAND'S CYRANO

The wine town of Bergerac[140] was another "must" on our list, to visit the Count of Bergerac, Edmond Rostand's *Cyrano*. The play *Cyrano de Bergerac* was performed for the first time in Paris in 1897 during the Spanish-American War.

Bergerac's small streets and squares were jammed! We took a picture of Cyrano's statue and left. However, it was the poet and dramatist[141] Rostand I was interested in—the man who created the swashbuckling swordsman—swaggering, heart-tugging Cyrano, with his huge feathery, white plume, bristling mustache, and long nose. Rostand inherited his fascinating imagination and flair for words from his Spanish Andalusian grandmother. Referring to Sarah Bernhardt, he said, "The beauty of her voice causes nightingales to die in despair." In the poem *Sacred Wood*, Greek gods dancing joyfully in the woods on Mount Olympus are interrupted when a twentieth-century automobile screeches onto the scene and two passengers climb out.

Rostand spent his early childhood in Marseille, then moved to Paris, where he studied law and married the perfect wife[142] for a sensitive, idealistic poet. When overwhelmed by man's insanity, Rostand found consolation in nature. Chanticleer, the rooster in his allegorical play *Chanticleer*, is everywhere at Rostand's beautiful home in Combo les Bains in the French Basque country. Chanticleer is the main character in the play. The cast consists of birds and barnyard animals, each with different personalities. The leading lady, Pheasant, is a temptress who is jealous of the dawn. "You are nothing to the dawn. You are all to me."

---

[140] Twenty-six miles south of Perigueux.

[141] His play *Les Romanesque*, based on Shakespeare's *Romeo and Juliet*, was adapted to the musical *Fantastics*.

[142] Rosemonde Gérard, poetess.

But Chanticleer sings to the sun, "You smile and soap suds glisten like a gem ... you make the sunflower turn her yellow head."

Rostand also found comfort in the Bible. His *Woman of Samaria* says, "This gracious Lord blesses the cursed, pities the poor and helpless, looks upon the least, loves the poor man, the child, the bird, the beast, the small sad donkey—wistful dogs we beat, and publicans ... and women of the street."

Rostand modeled Cyrano after a young writer living in Paris at the time of Louis XIII, Cardinal Richelieu, and the King's Musketeers. When the youth's wealthy father, who owned Castle Bergerac in the Chevreuse Valley, stopped his son's allowance, the idealistic rebel enlisted in the king's Guards. As part of his duties, his captain assigned him to write letters to the captain's wife.

Rostand wrote *Cyrano de Bergerac* for a cynical, disillusioned French society to bolster their self-esteem—to give them pride, self-confidence, and high ideals. In the play, his Count Cyrano, a boastful swordsman and poet, is an elite Musketeer in King Louis XIII's Guards. Although Cyrano was secretly in love with his cousin Roxane from Bergerac, he couldn't tell her. "Me whom the plainest woman would despise. Me with this nose of mine which arrives so long ahead of me." Roxane, however, was in love with Christian, a handsome Musketeer she had only seen but never met. When she asks Cyrano to introduce her, Cyrano agrees, and ends up writing love letters to her (supposedly from Christian), pouring out his own love for her. "Even though you never know I gave it to you, only let me hear sometimes, all alone, the distant laughter of your joy."

Christian is killed in battle, and Roxane enters a convent, where Cyrano faithfully visits her for fourteen years. Cyrano, still with blustering bravado hiding his love, is destitute, venting his unhappiness on others. His friends worry. "His satires make enemies ... those bravados yet may strike down our swordsman"—which is what happened. Although concealing a head wound, he keeps his regular rendezvous with Roxane. During the visit, before he dies, Roxane realizes that it was Cyrano who had written Christian's letters, and it was Cyrano with whom she had fallen in love. Even to the end, Cyrano is the proud Gascon, given to hyperbole and panache: "Tonight when I enter before God, my salute shall sweep all the stars away. One thing without stain, unspoiled from the world in spite of doom, mine own, that is ... my white plume." Sad and melancholy at the end of his life, Cyrano kept up his heroic gusto lest the world know his suffering. The author Rostand suffered deep depression after visiting French battlefields during World War I. He died at fifty during the flu epidemic.

STE. FOY LA GRAND

Crossing the Dordogne, we spent the night in the town of Ste. Foy La Grande on the border of the peaceful Gironde and Dordogne Rivers. Once a pilgrimage center, the church of Ste. Foy has one of the highest and most beautiful needle-like spires in France. At our spacious turn-of-the-century Grande Hôtel, we dined outdoors in a candlelit Roman courtyard atmosphere. The owners are a friendly young girl and her husband who is the chef. He is also a baseball fan. His collection of memorabilia includes autographed baseballs and gloves from the Yankees and Dodgers.

The town and church are named for an eleven-year-old girl, Ste. Foy (Faith), who was martyred[143] in the fourth century. After her death in Agen, many miracles occurred at her tomb. Pilgrims came and the town prospered, but jealous monks in Conques, 120 miles away, schemed to steal her relics. One monk enrolled himself at the monastery in Conques, where he stayed for ten years to divert any suspicion. When the time was right, he stole the relics to return them to their rightful place, and again miracles occurred. During the Revolution, to hide the church treasures, the mayor divided them among the parishioners. When Republican soldiers came to seize them, the mayor said, "But we have already had our revolution! We had it last week. The citizens, fired with revolutionary zeal, took all the treasures, and you know how impossible it is to recapture anything taken by a peasant—especially a good revolutionary." When the Terror was over, the people of Conques dug out all the church treasures, including Ste. Foy's jeweled statue,[144] made to hold the bones of the little girl.

---

[143] Tortured by a hot brazier during the reign of Roman Emperor Diocletian.
[144] The ancient gold statue depicts her sitting in a jeweled chair.

After leaving Ste. Foy, we stopped at a gas station. A man there had taken a welder's helmet and arranged mirrors inside to view the solar eclipse, and he offered to let us look. We had forgotten all about the eclipse. Thanks to an empty gas tank and another caring Frenchman, *les Américains* saw the August 11 eclipse of the sun at Carollon, between Ste. Foy and Route A-10.

Looking at the Eclipse through the Gas Station Owner's Homemade Viewer

LYONS

From the Vendée, we drove to Nantes to leave our rental car at the railroad station, took a taxi to the Sunday Market to buy a special cheese (*Fromage Le Curé Nantais*), then went back to the station to catch a train for Lyons, birthplace of Antoine de Saint-Exupréry, who wrote *The Little Prince*. Our perfect Belle Epoch Hôtel Royal in Lyons (on Place Bellecour) was near the post office and tourist office. The famous Place Bellecour, though huge, leaves much to be desired. There were some trees at one end and a statue of Louis XIV, and that was it.

On a beautiful evening, we crossed the Bonaparte Bridge over the Soâne River to Old Town in order to find outdoor restaurants and the Cathedral of St. John (twelfth to fifteenth century) containing St. John the Baptist's jawbone. St. Louis IX is buried in the cathedral, and Marie de Médici married King Henri IV there (after a rough sea voyage from Florence, and an even more tempestuous journey from Marseille). In Lyons, their son, Louis XIII, nearly died from a ruptured colon. Louis XIII's wife and mother, who were not his favorite people, stayed by his side night and day for weeks.

After visiting all the churches we could find—St. Nizier, St. George, and St. Paul—it was dark and time to eat at one of the many lively, outdoor restaurants. Chez La Mère Brazier was a good choice. Lyons is rightly renowned as an epicure's mecca. The chicken we ordered had been fed with thyme and marjoram. Two pretty girls from Vancouver sat next to us. One was on her way to teach French in Switzerland. They were staying at the Hôtel des Artists on Place des Célestins, frequented by actors from the theatre directly across the square. On the way back to our hotel, the Palais des Beaux Arts and Hôtel de Ville were beautifully lit, and the walk along the Soâne River was meant for lovers. We saw only a few, but that was okay. We had seen enough in Paris to last the whole trip.

Back at our hotel, we wanted to celebrate, but there was no ice. Room service informed us the ice machine was "broke up." We had to walk across the enormous square, Place Bellecour, to a McDonald's. Then we settled down for the night. I pulled a real Murphy bed out of the wall, which I hadn't seen since New York City. This Goldilocks snuggled down and was soon sound asleep; "it was just right." Before leaving Hôtel Royal with memories of hazelnuts for breakfast, we took a picture of the beautiful Art Deco staircase spiraling from the top of the hotel to the bottom.

An American businessman stood at the reception desk with his laundry bag that hadn't been picked up. He didn't understand, "We do not do laundry on the Feast of Our Lady's Assumption." Maybe he worked with one of the American companies headquartered in Lyons— Hewlett Packard, Black and Decker, or Schering Plough Corporation.

Outdoors, it was pouring rain. It should have been easy to leave town, but it wasn't. We had gotten wrong directions. However, if we hadn't been lost, we never would have gone up La Fouviere Hill, where we saw The Basilica of Nôtre Dame overlooking the city, as well as an amphitheater built by order of Augustus Caesar in 15 B.C.

MONTÉLIMAR AND AN ITALIAN VILLAGE PRIEST

Montélimar in Provence is famous for nougat candy. In the twelfth century, England's Richard the Lionheart attacked the Adheimar castle for the fun of it on his way to the Holy Land, and Louis XIII gave the city to the Grimaldi princes of Monaco.[145] Opposite the tourist office is the restaurant Don Camillo. What was Don Camillo doing in France? He should be in Italy. In Giovanni Guareschi's novel *Comrade Don Camillo*, Don Camillo is the Italian village priest who delights in outwitting the town's Communist mayor, Peppone. The restaurant walls are painted with huge pictures of the little priest on his bicycle, dressed in a black cassock and broad-brimmed hat. With him is the confused Peppone. When we asked the girl at the tourist office why the restaurant was named Don Camillo, the answer was, "Why not?" Montélimar is about seventy miles from the eleventh-century Grignan castle, high on a rocky peak overlooking the plains.

CLUNY

We drove back to Lyons for another night at Hôtel Royal and left early the next morning for Taizé, an hour away. Again we made another unscheduled stop, this time at Cluny, in Burgundy, where the castrated monk Abelard spent his last two years. During the Middle Ages, Cluny was a famous center of monastic reform, with 314 monasteries and more than a thousand monks. For 250 years, Cluny was the chief center of religious influence throughout Western Europe. Next to the pope, the abbot at Cluny was the most important ecclesiastic in the Latin Church. Today a few ruins remain, and the stables have been converted into a stud farm. A few miles away, however, there is a new monastery where the missionaries are lay people.

---

[145] They held it until the Revolution.

TAIZÉ—A NON-DENOMINATIONAL MONASTERY

For years we had heard about a unique, ecumenical community in France called Taizé. Now we were here, an hour from Lyons, waiting while a girl driving a tractor crossed the road in front of the parking area. The monastery of Taizé was founded in 1940 by Roger Schutz, whose father was a Swiss Calvinist minister. Instead of following his father's dogmatic religion, he chose the example of his maternal grandmother, a Reformed Protestant who attended both Protestant and Catholic churches.

Brother Roger studied theology in Strasbourg and Lausanne, but when his sister nearly died, he forgot theology and prayed. Deeply impressed by her miraculous recovery, he vowed to spend his life helping people of all religions. At twenty-five, he and three friends bought a rambling old house and small farm in the little hamlet of Taizé, perched on a hilltop in beautiful Burgundy. The following year, on June 14, 1940, France fell to the Nazis. When the Gestapo entered Taizé, Brother Roger and his friends were in Switzerland helping Jews cross the border.

After the war, Roger and his friends returned to Taizé, where they lived in solitude for nine years. "In every person is a zone of solitude that no human intimacy can fill, and there God encounters us" (Brother Roger). Soon the first brother arrived. Then came others of different Protestant denominations. Twenty years later, the first Catholic brother joined them, followed by a Catholic priest.

By 1952, the monastic community needed a rule. The monks followed the guideline of the Benedictine Order: work, prayer, celibacy, and communal property. In *Parable of a Community,* Brother Roger wrote, "The main themes are to bear the burdens of each other and accept whatever hurts each day brings, so you are concretely in communion with the sufferings of Christ. Be a sign to others of joy and brotherly love." As post-war Communism spread, the community grew. Members traveled as tourists in Eastern Europe, quietly setting up prayer circles in Poland, Hungary, and East Germany.

The day we visited Taizé, a beautiful, twentyish girl from Poland with blonde hair and brown eyes greeted us at the visitors' center. She had been coming for five years, and stayed six weeks each summer. She showed us a copy of their bi-monthly newsletter, which is translated into fifty-eight languages—including twenty-three Asian and seven African languages. She translated an advertisement in a German newspaper from the Brothers of Taizé:

Even though Clea seems to be a pretty girl to the outside, however, I have great concern about her ideas to master the hardships of life. So many succumb to the pressures of daily life—no commitments. Always afraid. And television helps it along by sending horror pictures into the house. I know an antidote. The little town of Taizé in Burgundy. There, young people from all over the world meet at the local monastery. No luxury. Sleep in tents, meals simple, water cold. Lots of rest. Listen to priests, pray—whoever wants—talk to each other. You get to know each other. Perhaps your fiancé gets a different attitude there.

The ad works. During the month of July, three thousand people from twenty different countries came to Taizé searching for answers. A young man from Slovenia, an economics student, confessed, "First I loved the music because I play the flute. Now I understand young people need God. This is the time we must decide about life, so we need calm inside." Another fellow from Italy said, "People just come to pray. It is important for people to come here and be accepted without having to say whether they believe or not. Taizé makes it possible for Christians of all denominations and even Hindus and Muslims to revere God." A scholarly-looking youth from Nigeria told us no gifts or donations are accepted. The ninety monks from different countries and religions keep the community self-supporting with a printing press, pottery, and a farm co-op.

Since it was nearly time for the 12:30 midday service, our Welcome Committee directed us to the Church of Reconciliation, a cement building that resembles an airplane hangar. Already the large hall was crowded with young men and women sitting on the floor. I squeezed in somewhere, and my two friends were lucky to find a spot nearby. Everyone wandered in quietly by themselves, although next to me, three girls with knapsacks came together. There was absolute silence for nearly ten minutes. Brother Roger and three other monks in white robes entered from the front and sat on small, wooden, fold-up prayer stools. We had been given blue song books with the words of each song translated into different languages: Latin, French, English, Spanish, German and Greek. Each quiet, reverent song of praise and petition (e.g., *Kyrie Eleison, Lord Have Mercy)* was followed by another period of silent meditation. Suddenly, the forty-five-minute service was over, and as silently as they had entered, two thousand people went their different ways. A small choir remained singing as we investigated the lit red candles on the left of the church. Each candle, symbol of the Resurrection and hope, was wrapped in red cellophane. This is where Russian, Greek, Romanian, and other Orthodox pilgrims celebrate their liturgy. A Russian priest visiting Taizé had brought his special altar, a piece of fabric containing the relic of a martyr. Nearby is an icon of the Virgin and Child.

We were so pleased with ourselves for having participated in such a beautiful service, we headed for the gift shop to buy a souvenir of Taizé: a flat cut-out silver dove suspended on a thin cord. The girl from Canada behind the counter said one of the messages is "Trust"—an awareness of the Holy Spirit.

A trail at the top of a hill overlooking lush fields led us downward to a lovely lake. The only trouble was obeying signs requesting silence. For me, that was tough. Since by then we were hungry, we followed our routine—find a scenic spot, sit down, and pull out leftover cheese, fruit, bread, wine, and chicken. While we ate, we watched others walking down the Silence Path. Some carried their fold-up stools attached to backpacks and used them to sit on while reading or sketching. Away from the quiet zone, a small group of girls and guys from different Balkan countries talked, laughed, and gestured. We also saw many older couples. As we left, it was lunchtime for the pilgrims, who sat on benches balancing plates of hot dogs and beans on their laps.

When Pope John Paul II left Taizé after visiting his old friend, Brother Roger, he told him, "One passes through Taizé as one passes close to a spring of water. The traveler stops, quenches his thirst, and continues on his way." That is what we did, hoping that church and government leaders who argue about past grievances will listen to the message of Taizé: "Focus on what unites people instead of what separates them."

5

ALSACE

COLMAR—THE WINE ROUTE
Frédéric Bartholdi (1834–1904)

THE TOURIST OFFICE in Colmar gave us information about the Wine Route and what to see, especially the home of painter-sculptor Frédéric Bartholdi (1834–1904), who designed the Statue of Liberty. After the Civil War in America, at a dinner party in Strasbourg, a French law professor, Edward de Laboulaye, proposed a memorial to celebrate the 100th anniversary of America's independence—a symbol of the friendship and alliance between France and America during America's struggle for independence. Bartholdi, a renowned sculptor, suggested the world's largest statue, "Liberty Enlightening the World." The dream, however, seemed doomed when Germany defeated France in the Franco-Prussian War, and Alsace came under German rule.[146]

During the war, Bartholdi came to America where he made sketches of Bedloe's Island, a dot in the New York harbor. Ten years later, a French-American Union was founded, and the dream was revived.

---

[146] During the Franco-Prussian War, Bartholdi was the liaison officer between Gambetta's French army at Tours and Garibaldi's headquarters in Dôle, knee-deep in snow.

Bartholdi would design the statue, and Gustaf Eiffel would design the iron framework. America would contribute the pedestal. Through thirty-eight years of traumatic difficulties and disappointments, Bartholdi's mother, who posed for the statue, kept the dream alive.

Although the statue was not completed for the centennial, they shipped the massive arm holding the torch of liberty to the Centennial Celebration in Philadelphia (August 1876), then back to Paris, where the head and shoulders were exhibited at the Paris Exposition in 1878. The gigantic statue, finally completed in 1884, was sent in sections to New York, where it was reassembled. Bartholdi was present when President Cleveland presided over the celebration.

Liberty's seven rays represent the seven seas. In her left hand, the tablet she holds is America's Declaration of Independence. Today her torch, which can be seen fifteen miles away, is still a symbol of hope welcoming immigrants to a new life. America, to Bartholdi, was the great pioneer that had paved the path of liberty for the entire world.

After World War I, Alsace was returned to France, but fell again to Germany in 1940. Still protesting their loss of liberty, defiant Alsatian women hung red, white, and blue sheets from bedroom windows and planted red, white, and blue flowers. Bartholdi's birthplace, 30 rue des Marchands in Colmar, is now a museum, but the town—with its plethora of gingerbread houses and little costumed dancing people on towels, tablecloths, and postcards—is too much. John Wayne never could have stayed here.

KAYSERBERG
Missionary Albert Schweitzer (1875-1965)

We left for Kaysersberg down the road—another Hansel and Gretel town with pretty girls in native costumes: black dirndl dresses, white lace aprons, and huge black velvet bows in their hair. It was such a beautiful day. Even a sunflower was wearing sunglasses.

The famous organist and missionary doctor Albert Schweitzer was born in Kaysersberg, but his family moved a few months later to Gunsback, fifteen miles away. Schweitzer's birthplace, now a museum, displays African artifacts, pictures, and an organ presented by the Paris Bach society. Photographs show him in Africa with three assistants and his patients in front of a converted chicken-coop hospital. Other pictures show Parcifal, his pet pelican, and his cat Sisi (who has parked herself on his writing desk), but most photos give a vivid picture of his working conditions in the primitive jungle.

He was one of four children. His mother was a missionary's daughter, and his father was a music teacher. At twenty-one, Schweitzer had decided he would study music and theology until he was thirty, and then devote his life to the poor. While studying and playing the organ at St. Sulpice in Paris, he heard about Sulpician missionaries in Africa. From then on, there was no more indecision about his career. He became a missionary doctor in the jungle of French Equatorial Africa (today's Chad), the Congo, Gabon, and the Central African Republic. When he needed a translator for different African tribes, God sent him a patient who had been a cook for European settlers. Using his professional vocabulary as a chef, he would translate and inform Dr. Schweitzer that "The man has pains in his right leg of mutton," or "This woman has pains in her upper left cutlet and in her fillet."

Dr. Schweitzer's wife, a nurse, accompanied him to Africa, but during World War I, since Alsace was ruled by Germany, they were considered "the enemy" and shipped to prison camps. The first was near Pau in the Pyrenees. The next was near St. Rémy in Provençe, where they became so sick they were sent back to Alsace.

After the war, to raise money for a new hospital in Lambarene, Dr. Schweitzer gave organ recitals, wrote books, and lectured on "The Reverence of Life." In 1953, at seventy-seven, he received the Nobel Peace Prize. He died in Africa at ninety-nine in his jungle hospital, still caring for the most destitute among men.

We stayed overnight down the road at Kientzheim, another fairytale village. Each building is a different pastel color, as if ice cream vendors had been hired to paint the town; strawberry here, pistachio there. Here a lemon, there a cherry. No wonder they wanted happy colors. After World War II bombings, one town in Alsace with 184 houses had only four left in ruins.

Our Hôtel l'Abbaye d'Alspach was a former convent of the eleventh-century Order of St. Claire of Assisi. My former nun's room is now decorated with matching designer draperies and bedspread. Each room with a balcony has a little patio separated from the next room by a white picket fence. The white chairs and table are plastic. (It rains a lot.) In the morning, birds chirped, whistled, and shrieked to wake us up in time to see a gorgeous sunrise. The rest of the day we dodged showers. At dinner that evening we drank Pinot Grigio[147] wine from traditional Alsatian green long-stemmed glasses, and ate trout, fluffy sauerkraut, goose stuffed with smoked sausage and chicken, and mushrooms cooked in wine. Alsatians throw Riesling wine into everything—meat stew, fish stew, etc. For dessert, there was *tarte flambé* and raisin cake.

As we sipped the region's special *digestif*, fruit brandy (*l'eau de vie*), a friend regaled us with childhood memories of her grandfather, who took her to pawn shops to buy whatever she wanted. When she was tired of playing with her purchase, they brought it back to the pawn shop and bought something else. The next day, as we drove from Kientzheim to Riquewihr, lush, green grapevines on each side of the road flowed forever toward the horizon. Even my California Napa Valley friend was impressed.

RIQUEWIHR

A gentle rain accompanied us to the enchanting, medieval wine town of Riquewihr. Tourists holding umbrellas strolled in and out of shops on the main street, but most were looking for a vacant seat in a restaurant. It was so crowded people ate outdoors on patios, holding umbrellas in one hand and forks in the other. Off the main street where geraniums tumbled from window boxes, we found Restaurant L'Arbaletier, *classé monument historique*, a cellar restaurant with warm, Old World ambience, a stained glass Art Nouveau window, and a young waiter with a grape-leaf designed necktie. He said he bought it at the marketplace in Strasbourg, but he should have bought a dozen. He could have sold them.

---

[147] From the grape, Pinot Blanc. Another variety is Riesling.

Riquewihr's town symbol, the Dolder Museum, is a thirteenth-century belfry. Another time, we will tour the château of the Dukes of Wurtemberg, along with the Hansi[148] Museum, dedicated to the World War I writer, cartoonist, and defiant French Resistance Fighter—if it doesn't rain.

RIBEAUVILLE

In Ribeauville a few miles away, we saw a stork's nest—a huge pile of sticks high in a tree. We were lucky to see even one. Since the marshes have been drained, storks are disappearing. No longer can they hunt frogs and other food for their young.

Ribeauville, like Kaysersberg, had recently been awarded honors in a nationwide contest, *Ville Fleurs*. Villages and cities in France compete in a contest for year-round flowers, open-air spaces, and environmental improvement (cleanliness of highways, public spaces, and city property). Too bad they didn't include dog-doo. We took turns wiping it off our shoes in picturesque, ancient fountains.

MONT STE. ODILE

From the wine country, we drove in the rain to Mont Ste. Odile, thirty-three miles from Strasbourg. The wind was blowing, and the rain was raining, but the elements never bother French people. Even on weekdays, people park cars and trudge up the mountain to visit the convent of Ste. Odile, patron saint of Alsace and the blind.

When Ste. Odile was born in the seventh century, blind and weak, her father, Duke Adalric, was so enraged, he killed the messenger who brought the news—his own son. To save the child from her murderous father, Odile's nurse fled with her, raised her in secret, and had her baptized. When she was confirmed, she recovered her sight. In answer to Odile's prayers, her father finally agreed to recognize her, on the condition that she marry a certain knight. When she refused, again she had to flee. Then another miracle—a rock split open providing refuge from her father's soldiers. This time, the duke gave her his summer residence, which crowned the mountain above his castle in Obernai.

---

[148] His real name was Jean-Jacques Waltz.

Ste. Odile converted the castle into a convent, and today, twelve centuries later, Mont Ste. Odile is a world-famous pilgrimage centre. When we were there in time for Mass, we met three ladies from Strasbourg who brought us to a cafeteria filled with visitors including a Boy Scout Troop and a group of Japanese tourists armed with cameras.

One of the Strasbourg ladies, a retired nurse, gave us a tour, starting in the huge, stainless-steel kitchen, then out into the rain, ducking in and out of different chapels. First, the eleventh-century Romanesque Chapel of the Cross, with Ste. Odile's father's sarcophagus below a large crucifix. (Before he died, he became a Christian.) Next, Ste. Odile's Chapel where her relics are kept behind an iron railing. In the Chapel of Tears, a worn stone slab in front of the altar is where she knelt to pray for her father's conversion. St. Michael's Chapel is vibrant with newly-restored mosaics that cover every inch of the walls and ceiling.

For the next thirty minutes, we trooped through wet woods behind our guide, who carried a collapsible walking stick she made from an aluminum cane. Using it as a pointer, she identified every tree in the forest. She also showed us a moss-covered wall older than the Druids. The sad part of the hike was the site of an airplane crash[149] that occurred January 20, 1992, killing all eighty-seven passengers. The area is enclosed with barbed wire and covered with little wooden crosses. Our hike ended at a miraculous spring struck by Ste. Odile to quench the thirst of an old man accompanied by his blind son. The rain stopped, and an enormous half-circle rainbow stretched out over the sky, embracing three countries: France, Germany, and Switzerland.

---

[149] Flight A320 Air International.

6

THE FRENCH ALPS AND
ST. FRANCIS DE SALES (1567–1622)

OUR FRENCH TOUR included a visit to St. Francis de Sales in the French Alps. To retrace the steps of St. Francis, a seventeenth-century bishop of Geneva and patron saint of journalists,[150] you have to climb mountains. St. Francis traveled on a mule, horseback, and on foot. We rented a car.

St. Francis, a nobleman, was from the mountainous region of Savoy in the French Alps—at that time, a duchy between France and Italy. To please his father, he studied law and theology in Paris, Orléans, and Padua, but at an early age he knew his vocation was in the Church. In 1593, in the beautiful town of Annecy in the Haute Savoy, St. Francis was ordained a priest and assigned to the dangerous Calvinist Chablais district bordering Lake Geneva (Lac Leman)—John Calvin's territory, where Catholic churches had been burned, convents closed, and priests forced into exile. Staunch Calvinists opposed the pope, bishops, and all the sacraments except baptism and communion (only symbolic). Clergymen and special laymen monitored the faith and morals of the citizens, even the police, lawyers, and tradesmen. Those who resented government interference and the austerity of a stern, condemning God were

---

[150] Oblates of St. Francis de Sales. Tel. 410.398.3057.

exiled. In 1594, the Catholic dukes of Savoy recaptured the region and requested that the bishop allow priests to return.

The Church needed reforming in the sixteenth century, and John Calvin (1509–64) was one of the reformers.[151] St. Francis wrote, "We must ask God ... to reform the abuses that have slipped in through the conduct of the Church's ministers ... It is because of us." One reason for the non-Christian-acting clergy was the Church's method of recruiting clergymen. The youngest sons of the nobility were expected to enter the Church, whether they had a vocation or not. For instance, John Calvin had a title and income from a diocese at the age of twelve. When St. Francis became bishop of Geneva, he required rigorous exams and testing of the seminarians.

In 1602, the previous bishop of Geneva,[152] ailing in exile at Annecy, sent his assistant, St. Francis, to Paris to negotiate with French King Henri IV regarding the livelihood of the clergy. Although priests were now allowed in the district of Gex, how were they to live? All church property had been confiscated. In Paris, St. Francis preached and heard confessions from commoners and nobility, including Queen Marie de Médici's court at her chapel in the Louvre.[153] After hearing his sermon at St. André des Arts Church, the duchess of Montpensier wrote, "This orator of holy love pounces on his prey and seizes it." King Henri IV asked St. Francis to preach at Fontainebleau, then played a joke on his Huguenot friends—delegates from Geneva. He invited them to Fontainebleau to hear "their bishop" preach.

Returning to Savoy, at Lyons, St. Francis learned that Bishop Granier had died. Now he had the full burden of a bishopric. As a bishop for twenty years, St. Francis traveled thousands of miles to visit his parishes—always subject to commands by the dukes of Savoy—whether the assignment was in Paris, in the capital of Savoy, in Turin over the Alps, or in Rome.

In 1618, at fifty-two, he was again ordered to Paris to accompany twenty-five-year-old Cardinal Maurice of Savoy. St. Francis wrote, "I

---

[151] John Calvin died three years before St. Francis was born.

[152] Bishop Granier.

[153] He reminded them that the King of Glory does not reward his servants according to the offices they hold, but according to the love and humility with which they fulfill their offices.

no longer belong to myself—no freedom except what he allows me."
(He had to teach the cardinal French.) They traveled from Grenoble
to Lyons, where they boarded a barge for five days to reach Orléans.
"Sometimes the cardinal rowed and made me row with him."

In Paris, he preached and heard confessions at Église St. Nicolas
du Chardonnet, where he became friends with thirty-eight-year-old
Vincent de Paul, who admitted that before meeting St. Francis, he had
had a "rather cynical disposition."[154]

This time, St. Francis had been sent to help negotiate a marriage
between the thirty-one-year-old Prince of Savoy, Victor Amédée,
and French King Louis XIII's sister, fourteen-year-old Christiane
(King Louis was seventeen).[155] Negotiations for the wedding took ten
months because King Louis XIII was feuding with his mother, Marie
de Médici. He had arranged his sister's wedding without telling his
mother, and didn't even invite her to the wedding. This time, the good
bishop couldn't wait to get out of Paris. He said the court was "a nest
of wasps hovering above a dead body."

On the return trip to his diocese—over ice-covered mountains via
Grenoble and Chambéry in January—he suffered a kidney infection,
bronchitis, and open sores on his legs. He was so thankful to be back
in Annecy, he wrote, "At last here I am in my nest." The following
Sunday in his sermon, he quoted St. Paul: "We are marching but in the
manner of an invalid who after leaving his bed, finds that he has lost
the use of his feet, and in frail health no longer knows whether he is
healthy or sick." No sooner had he recovered than the pope ordered
him to Rome on another mission—to help name a Superior General
for the Benedictine Order. He left in May over St. Bernard's Pass,
the one Hannibal used with his elephants. Despite a painful kidney
infection, he stayed twenty days, returning by way of Turin, over the
Alps again. On August 17, he arrived in Annecy. Two months later,
he had to accompany Cardinal Maurice to Avignon for a meeting
with King Louis XIII. On November 8, he was back in a boat in icy

---

[154] At that time, Vincent tutored the three children of Emanuel de Gonbodi, general
of the Galley Ships. He was also chaplain for the Royal Galley Ships.
[155] His father, Henry IV, was assassinated in 1610, eight years previously.

winds on the treacherous Rhône River. In Lyons, still preaching[156] and hearing confessions, he stayed in the gardener's cottage at the Visitation Convent. Louis XIII arrived with his entourage and stayed two weeks. On Christmas Eve, St. Francis said midnight Mass and two more Masses the next day—one in the Queen's palace, where Place Bellecour is today. On December 27, his eyesight began to fail, and he collapsed. Four hours later, doctors arrived and concluded he had had a cerebral hemorrhage. They cauterized him three times on the forehead with a hot poker. St. Francis de Sales died in Lyons December 28, 1622, at fifty-five. A Calvinist minister in Geneva said of him, "If we honored any man as a saint I know no one since the days of the apostles more worthy of it than this man."

GRENOBLE TO GENEVA

Determined to follow St. Francis' footsteps, we followed him from Grenoble north to Geneva, over the highest mountains in France, in the summer. In the winter, St. Francis traveled through ice and snow. Grenoble, in the Dauphiné region, was part of St. Francis' diocese of Geneva. The area was named for the French king's eldest son, the dauphin, who, according to custom, inherited the territory. The last dauphin was Louis XI, the Spider King, who died in 1483. Three mountain chains, the Chartreuse, the Vercors, and the Belledonne, encompass Grenoble, the city on the Isère River where Jean François Champollion taught at the university and, later, deciphered the hieroglyphics on the Rosetta Stone. The best way to appreciate Grenoble is in the bubble-shaped cable car, surrounded by beautiful snow-covered mountains.

On this trip, I was in a wheelchair. At the Paris airport, someone with a luggage cart piled high with suitcases banged into my heel, which required eleven stitches. I'll spare you the gory details. It was all very dramatic, right in front of a busy restaurant. Oh well, I broke up that complacent scene for travelers whiling away time between flights.

We had taken the TVA from Lyons to Grenoble, where our Hotel Atria was practically connected to the railway station by a cement

---

[156] "A man is free to acquiesce or turn away from God. Man remains free to answer yes or no."

courtyard. By the time we got settled and ready for dinner, it was late, but the evening was balmy, and the outdoor table at Les Archer restaurant was perfect.

The next morning a trolley car half a block from the hotel brought us to the huge Place Grenelle (grain) with its fountain and carousel. From there we boarded *le petit train* for a thirty minute tour in English. After the tour, we spent the rest of the day checking out places we had passed. The Parliament building is on the site of the palace of the Dauphiné where Louis XI, the Spider King, lived when he escaped from his father[157] after plotting to overthrow him.

Across from the Parliament building is the Church of St. André where a plaque commemorates Calvinist François de Bonne, the most prominent leader of the French Huguenots (1543-1626). His title was duc de Lesdiguiere. He was a follower of King Henri IV and helped end the Wars of Religion. When he heard St. Francis preach to Catholics and Protestants in the chapel of Parliament, he converted to Catholicism. His palace in Grenoble, behind Jardin de Ville, now houses Musée Stendhal.

Hector Berlioz (1803-1869), Composer

Off place St. André, rue Berlioz is named for the composer Hector Berlioz, born thirty miles outside Grenoble in Côte St. André. His father, a doctor, supported him in medical school in Paris until Berlioz insisted on a career in music. Then his allowance was cut off. Mostly, Berlioz taught himself music, and, in order to eat, sang in a chorus. At twenty-seven, he fell in love with the glamorous Shakespearean actress Harriet Smithson, on tour in Paris from England. Their marriage five years later ended tragically. Harriet fell as she was getting out of a carriage and broke her leg. Berlioz, the musical genius, was never home—he was struggling for recognition and money to pay exorbitant medical bills. His wife, once the toast of Paris, gained weight and became an alcoholic. They had a son who rarely saw his father, but when the boy went off to sea, Berlioz wrote, "You have at least a father, a devoted brother, who loves you more than you seem to think, but who longs to see your character become firmer, your mind more decided ... Have you cleaned your teeth properly? I have enclosed some envelopes so

---

[157] King Charles VII. Thanks to Joan of Arc, who had him crowned king.

you can write to your aunt ..." You don't want to hear the rest of the story—it's too sad.[158]

Berlioz, famous for his innovative orchestration, used hundreds of singers and musicians for the first time. His Russian bass player had such lustrous black eyes, Berlioz asked him if he soaked them at night in olive oil. He gave grandiose performances from England to Russia. His *Symphonie Fantastique* was composed after falling in love with his future wife. Before he died at sixty-six, someone asked him, "How do you get up so early? Do you go to bed with the sun?" He replied, "At my age who else do you expect me to go to bed with?"

Deodat de Dolomieu (1750-1801)

On the right bank of the Isère in Grenoble, behind *Musée Dauphinois*, is the Institute of Geology (called The Dolomieu, named for the father of modern geology, Deodat de Dolomieu, from Dolomieu near Grenoble). In 1791, he wrote a paper describing the mineral dolomite, with its streaked, startling colors. In 1798, he accompanied Bonaparte to Egypt but became sick and had to come home. On the way back, in Naples, the Italians captured him and kept him in a dungeon for twenty-one months. While in prison, he wrote a famous treatise on mineralogy in the margin of his Bible. He used a piece of wood for a pen and soot from a lamp for ink. Napoleon freed him the year the book was finished in 1808, but too late. He died the same year.

Another place we visited in Grenoble was Place de Berulle, where the French Revolution started after King Louis XVI sent in troops and suspended the Grenoble Parliament. Furious people ripped the slates off roofs and hurled them at the troops in what is called the Battle of the Rooftops. The French Revolution started in Grenoble with the nobles and middle class. When they lost control, the mob killed them.

VIZILLE

In Vizille, ten miles south of Grenoble, Parliament met in 1788 to protest Louis XVI's tyranny. They met at a château that once belonged to St. Francis' friend and convert, the duc de Lesdiguieres, who had ruled the

---

[158] His son died in Havana at thirty-three.

Dauphiné between 1616 and 1617. In our rental car, we arrived at Vizille at 5:00 p.m., closing time for the château. The château was the meeting place for Parliament when the "no taxation without representation" resolution was made. It began a national movement that ended in the French Revolution of 1789. Vizille prides itself on being the cradle of the French Revolution. In front of the château, with its magnificent staircase and ornate gate, stands an equestrian statue of the duc de Lesdiguieres. Inside the impressive wrought-iron gate, the four-acre park has lakes, a waterwheel, trees, flowers, birds, and animals—all in a cool, shaded, sylvan setting. It is nature at its best for parents and their beautiful well-behaved children, as together they watch schools of fish scooting in the water. Before leaving, we stood in line outside the gate at a food stand with all the happy French people on vacation, and bought chocolate walnut crêpes we're still dreaming about.

BASILICA OUR LADY OF LA SALETTE

The next stop was the Basilica of Nôtre Dame de la Salette near Corps.[159] The guide book cautioned us to avoid "The caterpillar trail of tourists and campers." Ha! No way could we avoid the pretty green area on the map (*les Montagnes*). We spiraled up a mountain halfway to heaven. At the top, a towering Romanesque-Byzantine basilica and monastery stand silent and alone in a mysterious setting surrounded by majestic mountain peaks. The basilica is dedicated to Our Lady of La Salette, who appeared here in 1846 to two children tending their cows—a boy, Maximin Geraud, age eleven, and a girl, Melanie Calvat, fourteen. The children saw a beautiful lady in a long, blue dress seated on a rock, crying, with her hands covering her face. When she stood up, they saw on her breast a crucifix with a hammer on one side and a pair of pliers on the other. A chain of roses was draped around her shoulders.

Speaking to the children in their mountain dialect, she told them she was Our Lady of La Salette. The hammer represented sin that drove the nails into her Son on the Cross. The pliers represented faithful love that can withdraw the nails. She said God is gravely displeased with the prevalence of sin and that, because of sin, calamities threatened France and all Europe.[160]

---

[159] Route de Gap. Excursions from the town of Corps 43 miles from Grenoble.
[160] Today the Church prefers to ignore warnings, choosing to emphasize God's mercy

She told the children that her Son on the Cross had given her to all men in every generation to be their Mother and intercessor, but "if my people refuse to submit to Him, I will be forced to let go the arm of my Son. It is so strong and heavy. I can no longer hold it back. If I want my Son not to abandon you, I am obliged to plead with Him constantly." If mankind continues to reject Him, all her efforts are in vain. She said she weeps because "His people have forgotten Him and His sacrifice on the Cross for their sins. I insist on unceasing prayers. My Son is not an avenger. He is a God of mercy and forgiveness."

She warned of famine. If His people are converted, "rocks and stones will turn into heaps of wheat, and potatoes will be self-sown in the fields ... Well, my children, you will make this known to all my people. Reform your lives and believe in the gospel." The beautiful

toward penitent prodigal sons and daughters.

lady, the reconciler of sinners, went up the hillside, rose a few feet from the ground, and disappeared. The Holy Spirit took over, and the uneducated children wrote her message to Pope Pius IX.

For five years, the children were subjected to humiliation, reprimands, and insults. Finally, the bishop of Grenoble gave the apparition official recognition. To celebrate, on September 19, 1851, fifty to sixty thousand people trudged up the steep mountain in a cold rain and stood in line for five or six hours to confess their sins to two old, ailing priests. The next year, three missionaries stayed in a cabin hearing confessions. In 1852, the eighty-seven-year-old bishop was determined to lay the cornerstone for a basilica to honor Our Lady. From Grenoble, it was a long, bumpy ride in a stagecoach. On the return trip, the old bishop had to be carried in a litter down the slippery mountain.

As for the children, Melanie entered a convent at the age of eighteen, where, as a celebrity, she "went Hollywood." She loved the limelight and became so obnoxious that visitors were forbidden. She went from one religious house to another, wearing first one habit, then another. She died in Italy in 1904 at seventy-two, an old, impoverished lady, alone in a rented room.

With no education or skill, Maximin couldn't hold a job. He, too, was in and out of seminaries. During the Franco-Prussian War (1870–1872), he served in the barracks in Grenoble, but he suffered from asthma and had to return home to Corps, where he died at forty. He is buried outside Grenoble in the Grande Chartreuse Monastery.[161] Before Maximin died, he said, "La Salette is now like a plant which in winter is covered with muck and manure, but when summer comes, it will bloom all the more beautiful for that very reason."

We had arrived at the basilica at twilight. Inside, a door led into the monastery, where we found two young seminarians—one from Paris, the other from Krakow. We were the first Americans they had ever met. We had a happy time chatting about Paris and the new Polish saint, Faustina, but it was time to leave.

Outside the basilica to the right is a miraculous spring that, until the apparition, was dried up. Since then, water has flowed constantly.

---

[161] A contemplative Order founded by St. Bruno from Rheims and six Carthusian monks.

Below the basilica, a circular, winding path leads to a statue of Our Lady of La Salette and the two children. A few pilgrims were there saying the rosary.

Twisting down the mountain around perilous curves in our comfortable car, we should have felt humble thinking about those early pilgrims trudging up this mountain—but we didn't. It was more like, "Dear God, please get us down from here before dark." It was so late when we returned to Grenoble that we ordered room service. The same headwaiter I had ignored the night before (he insisted I sit somewhere I didn't want to sit) was now all smiles as he brought us white wine and an assortment of appetizers and sponge cake, *gâteau de Savoie*.

ST. PIERRE AND ST. HUGHES

The next morning, after thanking God for our window view of mountain peaks, we left for two other places where St. Francis preached. The first was St. Pierre de Chartreuse, named for Savoy's patron saint. The pretty ski resort is nestled at the foot of snow-capped mountains. After visiting the church and the Chapel of the Rosary, with its statue of Mary and Baby Jesus above the church bell, it was time for lunch. At an outdoor patio, eighteen-year-old Sylvian, who is studying to be a mechanic, was our delightful waiter. He made St. Pierre a happy memory—but not the restaurant owner. When my foot fell in a hole in the uneven, broken stone floor, my dramatic reaction scared his pet parrot. It was all my fault when the parrot refused to eat his cracker.

Two miles south of St. Pierre, the tiny town of St. Hughes de Chartreuse is named for a young eleventh-century bishop of Grenoble. He found the perfect place in the Chartreuse Mountains for a secluded monastery. The little hamlet of St. Hughes is internationally famous for its contemporary sacred art, executed by one man, Jean Marie Pirot, known as Arcabas. We had come a long way to see his artwork in the small St. Hughes chapel. Guess what! It was closed (on Tuesdays). Fortunately, the door of the vestibule was open, and, through a second huge glass door, we could see Arcabas' innovative work depicting scenes from the gospels and the life of Christ. The chapel glows with brilliant shades of gold, orange, and red.

Paintings of *The Last Supper*, *The Resurrection*, and *Moses' Law* are on an upper level of the walls. Below the paintings is the artist's representation of Psalm 150:1: "Praise the Lord in his sanctuary. Praise Him in his mighty heavens." Stained glass windows, the tabernacle, tapestries, statues, the altar floor, engravings, and studded doors reflect the artist's personal praise. Outside, we met a photographer who had come from Spain—also on the wrong day. Our consolation prize for the closed door was a parade of cows with clanking cowbells coming home.

ANNECY
CHARTREUSE MOUNTAINS, LAKE ANNECY AND TALLOIRES

The drive to Annecy through the beautiful Chartreuse Mountains during holiday time in France was filled with challenges and construction. Our navigator, with a haphazard road map, finally gave up. "What? Another *perturbation*?" (traffic jam). She even made up a poem. "Route 205 or 203, whatever you decide to be."

Beautiful Annecy, with its lovely lake, was headquarters for St. Francis when he was bishop of the diocese of Geneva.[162] Annecy is also where St. Francis de Sales, with Ste. Jane de Chantal, established the first convent for the Visitation Order of nuns in 1610.

Our perfect Hotel Carlton in Old Town was across from a little park. As usual, first things first—find a romantic place to eat. The outdoor restaurant, Auberge du Lyonnais, is one of the many restaurants lining the quay of the Thiou canal that runs through town. All evening, people paraded along the path between the canal and the restaurants, with their twinkling lights and flower boxes. A continuous stream of lovers, young families, and tourists passed our table. Most were interested in strolling. Others stared at our food.

The next day, we boarded a boat for Talloires, at the other end of Lake Annecy, to see the ninth-century Benedictine abbey. Once, its gun-toting monks served as protection against barbarians. By the sixteenth century, the old abbey really needed reforming. St. Francis de Sales did that. Today, it is a four-star hotel, Hôtel

---

[162] 1602–1622

l'Abbaye. In the lobby, an enormous *trompe d'oeil* shows the backs of a procession of hooded monks. The bar downstairs was once the monks' wine cellar.

Hôtel l'Abbaye, on a sheltered, gently curved bay, is one of the many beautiful lakeside spots in France. We ordered drinks at a table in a little grove of trees overlooking the lake and watched swarms of paragliders soaring in the blue sky. A statue tucked among the shade trees commemorates the French chemist, C. L. Berthollet, who was born here (1748–1822). One thing he proved is that chlorine is bleach. Barthollet went to Egypt with Napoleon, but after Napoleon's defeat, he welcomed back King Louis XVIII.

To see what the real world looked like, we walked (I was still being pushed in a wheelchair) up a winding slope behind the hotel and found vacation apartments with bright, colored flowers spilling over railings, men playing boules, and families with many children sunbathing around a swimming pool in a park.

We also found the Church of St. Mary, once called the Hermitage of St. Germaine. St. Francis came here on a retreat the year before he died. He said, "My soul ... is like a clock that is out of order; it must be dismantled piece by piece, and after it has been cleaned and oiled, it must be reassembled to make it chime more accurately." Relics of fifth-century St. Germaine are buried under the altar. Twice, St. Germaine was sent to Britain from Gaul, and once he saved a small British army from the Picts and Saxons by leading the British to a narrow ravine between two high mountains. When the enemy came, he told the British to shout "Alleluia" three times as loud as they could. Echoes magnified their shouts, and the invaders, thinking they were outnumbered, fled. The Church has always been "Militant" until recently.

The boat back to Annecy made several stops to pick up or drop off passengers at different towns along the lake. Back in pretty Annecy, we walked through the public garden, inspecting flowers, fauna, and a great variety of trees, each marked with its name. Our favorite was a weird yew tree. We decided nature is a universal language, uniting people through beauty. A young "Figaro" had just struck up a conversation with a pretty girl. Frantic because he didn't have a pen to write her address, he rushed over to us to ask if we had a pen he could borrow. Yes, we did. Off he flew to the girl, pulled out a scrap of paper, scribbled on it, and ran back to return the pen just as the girl was walking away. I don't think his chances for a date were very good.

Next, we looked for churches where St. Francis had preached, mostly about the sin of gossip. All the churches in Annecy, and most churches throughout France, were destroyed during the French Revolution, but the majority have been restored. The Church of St. Francis de Sales is now an Italian church with a baroque altar, roses, lace, and a statue of an ancient black Madonna. Another statue honors St. John Bosco from Italy (1815–1888), who started the Salesian Missionary Order of priests in Turin to help homeless boys. With his widowed mother as housekeeper, he built schools, workshops, and churches. By 1856, he had a family of 150 boys. Later he founded a home for destitute girls.

The Church of Nôtre Dame de Liesse (Rejoicing) has a plaque outside that says St. Francis' mother (age fifteen) prayed here and made a vow to the Virgin that if her unborn child should be a boy, she would consecrate him to God. That was St. Francis. When he became bishop, he preached here. "Look at the bees. They suck bitter juice from thyme, and by their nature convert it into honey. Devout souls find many hardships, it is true, but in accepting them, they convert bitterness into sweetness."

The Cathedral of St. Peter has a very dramatic altar with soft, golden light behind white marble statues, but when St. Francis was ordained a bishop, the church was small and dark. His sermons were always of a merciful God, "… but you must obey His commandments. Otherwise you can never be happy. God will never reject you unless you reject Him." One hundred years later, Jean Jacques Rousseau (1712–1778),[163] who introduced the slogan, "Liberty, Equality, and Fraternity," played the flute and sang in the cathedral choir here. The bishop's house is now the National School of Music next to a police station.

---

[163] Rousseau, at sixteen, was an apprentice to an engraver in Geneva. Badly treated, he ran away from his Calvinist home.

Opposite the Town Hall on rue Joseph Blanc, the Church of St. Maurice is named for a third-century Egyptian officer in the Roman legion. He refused to make sacrifices to Roman gods, and at Martigny near Lake Geneva, he withdrew all his men from the army. Roman Emperor Maximin Herculius executed him and his entire legion of six thousand.

ANNECY ANCIENT CASTLE

Annecy's ancient castle, on a hill above Old Town, once belonged to the counts of Geneva, who fought off both the French and Spanish during Savoy's nearly three-hundred-year[164] reign as an independent state. When we visited, the enormous courtyard inside the castle was filled with artists and their easels.

In 1600, the duke of Savoy, Charles Emmanuel, was at war with French King Henri IV, who sent French troops to occupy Savoy. A truce was finally signed, permitting Catholics to worship in three parishes of Gex. When King Henri IV came to Annecy in 1601, he brought his mistress, Marquise de Verneuil. They stayed at the castle and invited the embarrassed Bishop Granier to dinner. Later that year, the bishop sent St. Francis to Paris to persuade the king to help priests in Gex. After ten months, he returned with empty promises.

The castle overlooks the old, medieval town paved with cobblestones. I was still in the wheelchair, with a free ride up and down streets bordered by shops and restaurants. On the main street, St. Claire, we searched for Le Freti Taverne. We finally found it in a twelfth-century home that advertised "cheese and wine upstairs." Upstairs? No way. We ate at one of the restaurant's sunny, outdoor tables on the street and, again, watched happy crowds coming and going. We also learned that *l'avaret* is a fish.

On our last day in Annecy, we visited the Basilica of the Visitation at the top of the steep hill where St. Francis and Ste. Jane de Chantal are buried. The view of snow-capped mountains, the lake, and the town is magnificent.

---

[164] 1416–1714.

BASILICA OF THE VISITATION AND STE. JANE DE CHANTAL (1572–1641)

Ste. Jane de Chantal from Dijon, a wealthy thirty-one-year-old widow, was not looking forward to spending the rest of her life with nothing to do but pray and worry. The Holy Spirit took care of that, and today she is the patron saint of vocations.

Her religious father, a lawyer and president of the Burgundian Parliament in Dijon, invited her to visit him for Lent to get her away for a few days from her irascible seventy-year-old father-in-law, Baron Guy de Rabutin, with whom she lived with her four children. He had threatened to disinherit her children if she didn't live with him. Also living with them was the baron's mistress-housekeeper and her five illegitimate children.

Ste. Jane de Chantal stayed in the run-down, gloomy estate at Monthélon near Autun for eight years during a time of famine and epidemics caused by religious wars. In back of the castle, she kept bread in an outdoor oven and a huge pot of hot soup for beggars standing in line with their soup bowls. She used the attic as a makeshift hospital to treat people, including lepers and prostitutes with dreadful diseases. She made ointments from herbs, and when patients died, she washed them and wrapped them in shrouds.

St. Francis met Ste. Jane de Chantal in Dijon in 1602, when he preached (at her father's invitation) a Lenten service in the chapel of the Burgundian Ducal Palace.[165] He knew when he saw her in her black widow's clothes that she was destined for the Church. He knew that someday they would together found an order of nuns to help the poor and sick. For six years, he corresponded with her as her spiritual adviser. She was inclined to be gloomy, and he had to constantly remind her to guard against anxiety, melancholy, and scruples: "Live joyously. Live from day to day ... avoid worry and discontent, which like a severe winter, strips the earth of all its beauty ... it deprives the soul of peace and happiness."

In 1607, he asked her to come to Annecy. At that time, he told her of his plan to start an order of nuns. He also told her that his mother hoped another son, Bernard, would marry Jane's eldest daughter,

---

[165] The Ducal Palace now houses the Town Hall and museum.

Marie-Aimeé. After Ste. Jane de Chantal returned to Dijon, her youngest daughter, Charlotte, died, and nine-year-old Marie-Aimeé was married to St. Francis' twenty-five-year-old brother. The following year, St. Francis' mother, Mme. de Boisy, with whom the little girl was to have lived, died. Since Ste. Jane de Chantal was now needed to care for her daughter (the child bride), she left Dijon again. This time she came to Annecy with her daughter, Françoise, along with the little bride and her godmother. Her sixteen-year-old son,[166] the eldest, was left under the guardianship of her father until he could enter the court of Marie de Médici. Her husband French King Henri IV was assassinated the year Ste. Jane de Chantal left for Annecy (1610) to found the order of nuns. The Order of the Visitation was named for the second Joyful Mystery of the Rosary, when the Blessed Virgin visited her cousin, Elizabeth.[167]

In seventeenth-century France, there was a great spiritual revival. Wealthy noblewomen with meaningless lives were taking vows of poverty, helping the sick, and bringing food and clothes to people living in wretched hovels. In Annecy, the Visitation nuns walked through the worst slums in town, but St. Francis, knowing the danger, ruled that the Sisters should be cloistered, while still providing food and medicine. Mainly, however, they worshiped God in song and prayer. Always, they stayed informed of worldly events and offered sacrifices in thanks, adoration, and reparation.

Ste. Jane de Chantal, like St. Francis, rode on horseback throughout France, over mountains and in all kinds of weather. Before she died at Moulins (2 ½ hours from Lyons) nineteen years after St. Francis died, she had established eighty-seven Convents of the Visitation. Today there are 165.

We left the wheelchair outside the door of the Visitation Basilica in Annecy, hoping no one would borrow it. The church is memorable for the twelve grey-and-white marble columns and chandeliers with clusters of big, glass globes. An enormous mosaic above the altar depicts the Trinity. St. Francis is buried on one side of the altar, and Ste. Jane de Chantel on the other. Stained glass windows illustrate their lives.

---

[166] Celse-Benigne. His daughter was Mme. de Sevigné.

[167] Elizabeth was the mother of John the Baptist.

Next to the basilica is a shop where books, postcards, and cassettes are for sale. Adjacent is a museum (inside an enormous boulder) with a ten-minute slideshow, photos of places the saints visited, and memorabilia, including Ste. Jane de Chantal's Book of Psalms that she carried in her saddle bag on her journeys. We gave the museum a quick glance because Sister Marie Thérèse, in her black habit, came from the bookstore to say it was closing time. Sister Marie Thérèse was our favorite souvenir of the Basilica of the Visitation, with her big, brown eyes and beautiful, happy smile. She might have been twenty-five or maybe not. With nuns, you never know.

THÔRENS

The next morning we left Annecy to visit St. Francis' birthplace outside the town of Thôrens. Thôrens is a pretty town, with flowers everywhere. St. Francis was baptized here, and in 1602 he was ordained bishop in the little church of St. Maurice. A statue of St. Maurice, the martyred Roman soldier from Egypt, stands above the front portal. The church was closed, but we could imagine St. Francis' proud family sitting in a front row and, behind them, all the Savoy nobility. To prepare for his ordination, he had spent twenty days alone at Château de Sales "to compose my poor spirit that is so disturbed by so many affairs."

While we were in Thôrens, I bought some badly-needed hair spray at a beauty parlor. The pretty girl who worked there left her male customer (who was getting a haircut) draped under a cloth while I pondered which brand to buy. A few doors away, at a combination smelly bar and ice cream parlor, a friend admired a poster advertising a horse race. The generous but forbidding-looking man gave it to her. To thank him, we bought Eskimo Pies on sticks.

CHÂTEAU DE SALES

Château de Thôrens is high above the valley of Thôrens, twelve miles from the town. Built over an eleventh-century fortress, the original castle had rambling buildings and a series of massive towers.

When Ste. Jane de Chantal and her two daughters visited St. Francis' mother here, she wrote, "Steep cliffs overshadowed the road. It rained all day. The mules picked their way along narrow paths with a rocky face on one side and a sheer drop on the other ... running into armies, making detours, traveling a whole week by paths that led us along the most frightening precipices imaginable."

The château where St. Francis was born was burned by Cardinal Richelieu[168] during the Thirty Years' War.[169] It has been rebuilt near the original site, complete with drawbridge. Our tour guide, a blond, eighteen-year-old boy, obviously loved his job. He was especially proud of a room dedicated to Premier Camillo Cavour, the first Prime Minister of Italy after the unification. He stayed here between 1852 and 1859. One of his descendants married into the de Sales family. The older wing of the castle is a museum with portraits and memorabilia of St. Francis' bishopric—vestments, chalice, miter, etc. Three walls of another stone room are covered with enormous tapestries.

After the tour, we sat on a bench to view the awesome, panoramic scene below—the same unspoiled view of the countryside St. Francis saw when he lived here. A stony path leads up a hill to the site of the original fortress. One friend decided, "These must be the ruins. They look ruined."

LA ROCHE SUR FORON

From the town of Thôrens, we drove to another town, La Roche, where St. Francis attended school for three years, from age five to eight. Years later, he returned to preach at the church of St. Dominic.[170] La Roche is also where St. Francis found a saintly woman with a rather "irksome" husband.

On the main street, lantern-shaped street lights dangle from medieval wrought-iron fixtures. La Roche was the first city in Europe

---

[168] 1585–1642

[169] The war began in Bohemia, but involved most countries in Europe as Catholics fought against Protestants. Then it evolved into wars for power that devastated Europe.

[170] St. Dominic was a 12th–13th-century Spanish priest who started the Dominican Order, famous for their intelligent sermons.

to have electric lights. On one side of the main street, a long row of outdoor tables was filled with young people hanging out. *Mon chauffeur* parked the car, then wound her way among the tables to get directions to the school. As usual, everyone wanted to help—which gets very confusing. By using lines and arrows drawn on the back of a paper plate, we found the school on top of a steep hill. Today, the school houses low-income families with many children. However, the enormous square in front of their doorstep is perfect for rollerblades. The view of the countryside is breathtaking, but not as impressive as little boys on bikes, pedaling effortlessly up and down steep streets, and lovers on motorcycles, kissing each other through their helmets.

CHAMBÉRY

Returning to Annecy for the night, we had intended to stop at Chambéry, where St. Francis preached, "Love will break open hearts of stone ..." but the traffic was, as they say in French, *formidable*. I wanted to see the chapel where the Spider King married Charlotte of Savoy without his father's permission. We drove past the cathedral that once housed the Holy Shroud of Christ's Passion before its final destination in Turin.[171]

We also found the famous Elephant Fountain. It is a very funny fountain. Four elephants, with their long trunks and two front feet, stick out from four sides of a column. The French call them *Quartre Sans Cul*, "Four Without a Rear End." The statue is dedicated to Comte de Boigne (1751–1830) from Chambéry, who enlisted in the Irish Brigade in France, served in the Russian army, and was captured by the Turks. He joined the East India Company in 1796 and eventually fought for the Hindustani. After British soldier-statesman Robert Clive defeated the French in India and returned to England, everyone vied for power. Comte de Boigne's military victories for the Hindustani made their ruler[172] master of northern India. When Comte de Borgne returned to

---

[171] By 1978, the shroud had crossed the Alps and been carted around since the 12th century to more than twenty-five places. A French crusader brought it from Constantinople to Lirey, France, near Troyes.

[172] Maratha Sinahais.

Chambéry in 1802 with a fortune and the rank of general, he practically rebuilt the town.

A statue is dedicated to the de Maistre brothers, Joseph and Xavier. Count Joseph de Maistre,[173] the elder brother, was a lawyer and writer until the Reign of Terror, when he fled to Lausanne, Switzerland. In Lausanne, he and the exiled writer[174] Mme. de Staël became friends. Both were brilliant and loved to discuss religion and politics. She was a Protestant republican, and he was a Catholic monarchist. Exchanging opinions was their favorite entertainment, a verbal game of ping pong. He told a friend, "Together we created scenes in Switzerland that would make you die laughing." But the fun ended when Joseph was sent to Russia for fifteen years as the Sardinian ambassador. After Napoleon's defeat, he returned to Savoy. His brother, Xavier de Maistre, who was nine years younger, fought against Napoleon with the Piedmont army, but when Napoleon conquered Savoy and Italy, he joined the Russians. Before leaving from Turin, Xavier was jailed for dueling, and amused himself by writing a popular fantasy *Voyage Autour Ma Chambre* (*A Journey Around My Room*). In St. Petersburg, after many battles, he was commissioned major general, and died there in 1852.

AIX AUX BAINS

At Aix aux Bains, a spa resort near Chambéry, we checked out the baths and beautiful homes, then drove back to Annecy. It was another perfect evening at a sidewalk table. This time we ate at L'Étage[175] restaurant on rue de Paquier. We ordered trout cooked in blue cheese and *poromier* (cabbage, spinach, and green pepper). Our table was practically attached to another table where a good-looking couple held hands and gazed into each other's eyes. One of my friends suddenly realized she had been eating their bread, and they didn't even notice. When they left, the glamorous, sophisticated girl was carrying her

---

[173] (1754–1821).

[174] They agreed on one thing: that a Satanic force menaces humanity at all times. Napoleon hated her. She wrote, "He is not a man but a system. He considers women only useful to produce conscripts for his future wars. Otherwise, they are a sex which he would like repressed ..."

[175] First floor.

motorcycle helmet. Directly across the street, a building with a wrought-iron balcony had a plaque that said it was built by the de Sales family in the sixteenth century and served as a residence for the dukes of Savoy when they visited. That evening we watched a spectacular fireworks display in the darkened sky over the lake.

CHAMONIX
—Mer de Glace (Sea of Ice)

Chamonix is a crossroad for France, Switzerland, and Italy. To get there, you drive over a high, scary bridge, then through a dark tunnel. As you emerge into daylight, Mont Blanc, like a tantalizing strip teaser, treats you to a sneak preview of her beauty—then back you go into another tunnel.

At Chamonix, we boarded a cable car packed with serious mountain climbers (with ropes wound around their waists and carrying other paraphernalia) to see the famous Mer de Glace (Sea of Ice). Mer de Glace is the largest, most beautiful glacier in the French Alps. The melting and freezing moves it as it rolls to the sea, sweeping thousand-pound boulders *very* slowly. Time is nothing to a glacier; it took twelve years to move a man's hat one mile.

On postcards, Mer de Glace is snowy white. In summer, it is a wide swath of brown dirt, but that was okay. The snow-capped mountain peaks and brilliant blue sky surrounding us compensated. We were prepared to be cold, but at the outdoor restaurant, Hôtel du Montenvers, it was so hot we kept moving our chairs to stay shielded under table umbrellas. The restaurant is a perfect people-watching place, as passengers spill out of the little cog train and others wait for the descent. We heard accents from all over Europe and, as always, Japanese. The family beside us was from Holland.

Lunch was *tapinade* (chopped olives), salmon, and "skin potatoes in their rolls," and, for the first time, we found *Vin de Savoie*. The label on the crisp, white wine has a white cross against a red shield, the Savoy emblem. The cheese was also *de Savoie,* round and thick on the outside, with soft, warm, cheese on the inside. It's called *sechée*, "edge of cheese in the oven." We watched children climb in and out of a hole in an enormous boulder, and practiced French on our good-natured waiter, a young man from New Zealand. *Sauvez ma place, s'il vous plaît* (Save my place, please). Every twenty minutes, newcomers in hiking boots arrived and headed for the narrow path up the mountain. They carried walking sticks and wore safari hats to protect the back of their necks from the sun. The most fascinating were the shirtless, wiry, sun-blackened men weighted down with heavy knapsacks strapped over bare skin.

To visit the ice cave, or Grotto de la Mer de Glace, either take the cable car or hike down the winding, hairpin trails. Stand in line, enter single file into an eerie world of ice, then dodge drops of water. Each room exhibits a different ice sculpture. We saw four easy chairs, a coffee table, a piano, a fireplace, and an enormous carved polar bear. From inside the cave, you can watch hikers descend a narrow, mountain path. You can also have your picture taken with two huge, shaggy St. Bernard dogs.

Out in the sunshine, we boarded the little train again. Descending the steep mountain, we passed mountain pastures that St. Francis wrote about. "I have encountered God very often in the calm and warmth that exists amid our highest and harshest mountains, where goats and chamoises[176] run hither and yon on the treacherous ice ... Oh what good people I have found among such high mountains." In St. Francis' sixteenth century, people cut off by snow and ice were superstitious and practically uncivilized. They had never heard of the Christian religion. "Poor widows and humble village women so productive, whereas bishops so highly elevated in the church of God are all ice ..."[177]

ST. GERVAIS

We left Chamonix and had dinner in another St. Francis town, a pretty spa town called St. Gervais.[178] To get there, we had to cross

---

[176] Rare Alpine antelopes that survive above 6,000 feet.

[177] A statue in Chamonix commemorates Dr. Michel Paccard, the first man to climb Mont Blanc (in 1786) with his porter Jacques Balmat—the latter a brave but pathological liar whose printed boasts convinced the world for 174 years that he, and not Dr. Paccard, was the first to climb Mont Blanc.

[178] A first-century martyr from Milan. Also martyred were his twin brother, Proteus, and their parents. In Paris, Église St. Gervais and Proteus are next to Hôtel de Ville.

the scary Devil's Bridge, *Pont du Diable*. We parked in a square behind the Town Hall. Fortunately, the nearby tourist office was open. There we learned that Mme. Curie had died here at the Sancellemoz Sanatorium in 1934, after a lifetime of exposure to radium. The town is famous for its baths (*les bains*), and an excursion train brings people to the snowy peaks of Le Nid d'Aigule (Eagle's Nest) and another glacier, Bionnassy. A Mountain Guide Festival (*Fête des Guides)*, is celebrated August 4–5,[179] and, lest we forget, St. Gervais, like Thorens and Thones, was the scene of desperate heroism by the *Maquis* (rural guerilla bands of French Resistance fighters) during World War II.

La Gaeta, the perfect restaurant on a beautiful August evening, was a reminder that St. Gervais is in the middle of very cold, dangerous mountains. The walls of the warm, dark-wooded interior are decorated with Alpine museum pieces: an ancient saw, a bow, skis, etc. Leaning over an enormous fireplace, a man spent the entire evening cooking meat and filling individual braziers[180] with hot coals. The waitress told us that during the war, hundreds of braziers were ordered for the Resistance, but instead they received hundreds of ladies' brassieres.

In the warm, friendly ambience, we found another "must" on our list, Savoy *raclette*—cheese served on a cast-iron plate with a handle attached to a brazier of hot coals. Slide the cheese close to the coals to melt it, and then push it back to scrape (*racler)* the softened cheese onto your plate. A good-looking couple sitting on an outside porch overlooking treetops was delighted to have their picture taken *"racletting"* the delicious cheese.

EVIAN

On the way to Geneva, we stopped at Evian, another spa town, famous for Evian mineral water. They produce fifty million bottles a month. The plant stretches for two or three city blocks. We drove along the shore of Lake Geneva, past the enormous Nautical Centre and the beautiful, shady,

---

[179] Each year a "Guides Day" raises money to help families of guides lost in rescue work.

[180] A metal pan for holding burning coals or charcoal.

English garden (*Jardin Anglais*), then parked near quai Charles Besson.[181] At an outdoor restaurant overlooking the lake, a glorious summer sunset decorated the sky. Our talkative, fiftyish waiter, originally from Canada, lives in Paris. The restaurant owners are his friends, and when he came to visit, they put him to work. He was like *The Man Who Came to Dinner,* who stayed and stayed. He had to leave us in a hurry because the owners were yelling at him to get back to work.[182]

GENEVA

The drive into Geneva at night is a romantic dream world, with softly-lit, elegant architecture and twinkling amber lights reflected in the water. We were fortunate to find a hotel. They were all booked for an unromantic wrestlers' convention.

The next morning, we drove along the shore of Lake Geneva (Lac Leman), with its geyser shooting rocket-like into the blue sky. We were on our way to Thonon-les-Bains, the largest of all the confusing "TH" towns in the Chablais district: Thones, Thorens, and now Thonon.

THONON-LES-BAINS

Newly-ordained St. Francis de Sales (1593) was assigned to convert souls here. The region was totally Calvinist. Four years before, the entire Chablais had been ravaged by French troops sent by Huguenot Henry of Navarre[183] against Catholic dukes of Savoy. Churches and castles were destroyed, Mass forbidden, and Catholics exiled. A priest's life was in danger, not only from bounty hunters, but also from wolf packs. At nearby la Chavanne, St. Francis escaped a wolf pack by climbing a tree and lashing himself to a limb with his belt. The only place he was safe was ten miles away in Allinges, in a fortress owned by a friend of his father. To say Mass every morning in the Catholic town of Marin, he had to cross the Dranse River in

---

[181] The port is in front of the English Garden. Boat trips to Lausanne (on the Swiss side) tour Lake Geneva day and night. The night cruise includes an orchestra and dancing.

[182] Evian boasts baths, a gambling casino, and an eighteen-hole golf course.

[183] Later, French King Henri IV.

all kinds of weather to reach a little chapel on the other side. One winter, when the bridge broke, he crawled across on an icy plank over roaring water. When the governor of Marin heard about it, he refurbished a chapel in an ancient convent on the opposite shore.

In Thonon, we found the church of St. Hippolytus,[184] where St. Francis preached. It is adjacent to the Basilica of St. Francis, but both were closed for repair. Although St. Francis wasn't permitted to say Mass there, he was allowed to preach after the Calvinist service. Only a handful stayed, but he spoke to them in language they understood, "When caught out in the fields by a storm, little bees pick up small stones so they can keep their balance in the air and not be easily carried away by the wind. So also when our soul has made its resolution and firmly embraced God's precious love, it keeps steady amid the inconstancy and change that comes from afflictions ..." In talks and pamphlets, he asked people to pardon one another and reminded them that Christ died to save all men, not just a favored few.

Today, Thonon-les-Bains is a summer spa resort on Lake Geneva. We ate lunch outdoors amid flowers and fountains on Place du Château, where the dukes of Savoy once owned a castle. Flowers surrounding the statue of a general who helped destroy the Bastille in Paris are changed daily to note each day of the month. Strolling through town, we saw a store window filled top to bottom with layers of different colored candies. From a shady park overlooking Lake Geneva, the spectacular view is as healing as the thermal baths. A funicular descends to the lake shore through gorgeous gardens bursting with blooms—mostly roses. On the little cog train, a blind woman alone with her white cane stepped aboard and walked as confidently as if she could see, but she couldn't—not the huge, tree-shaded picnic area, the double carousel, the string of boats bobbing in the water, nor the lovely roses. So sad.

To feel happy again, we bought some clothes. The salesgirl told us, *Tenez-vous vôtre temps* ("Take your time"). I bought a long, black, lace dress, and she said it would look wonderful with a

---

[184] Named for a third-century martyr who was banished by Emperor Maximus to Sardinia and died in 235A.D.

Wonderbra! As we drove through Geneva for one more night, we felt like 'atmosphere' on a movie set with glittering lights, five-star hotels, and rows of stretch limousines dispensing Arabs with their gorgeously-gowned women.

ALLINGES

The next day, still following St. Francis, we drove ten miles from Thonon up a mountain to the small town of Allinges, where St. Francis stayed while he commuted on horseback to preach at Thonon. We parked at the bottom of a hill in a beautiful meadow with trees and wildflowers, where the only sound was the chirping of birds, then walked up (by now I was walking) a steep hill to the half-crumbled walls of an old fortress. The caretaker, a gentle old man, showed us a video of St. Francis' journeys, then opened a door to our right. We stepped into a dark, tiny, old Roman chapel with a small stone altar and faded Byzantine frescoes. The stained glass windows on one side are thin slits in the stone wall. Eight ancient hand-carved, worm-eaten wooden benches are on either side of a narrow aisle. In winter, the freezing mountain temperature must be below zero, but Mass has been said here since the eleventh century.

One side of the Allinges fortress overlooks a panoramic view of the Chablais region. On the other side, the scenery is even more spectacular, with Lake Geneva in the distance. Hopefully, St. Francis had a chance to sit on the old beat-up bench here to enjoy the view. A path leads to his large statue at the top of a hill. I had a long one-way conversation with him before saying goodbye to the humble, serene saint who won converts with his amiable personality; who spoke simply and naturally without dramatic rhetoric; and who, somehow, found time to write twenty-six volumes, including two best sellers. His *Introduction to a Devout Life* says that monotony and jealousy are the two main enemies to marital happiness: "The Holy Spirit does not abide in a house where there are sharp retorts, bickering and arguments." (According to "Dear Abby," the columnist, the main enemies are sex and money.)

As we left the site of the old fortress, we noticed a sign at the back of the building advertising an art exhibit. The artist, Capucine Mazille, was there to tell us about her hilarious, imaginative paintings. Remember her name.[185] Her next exhibit will be in San Francisco.

BLÉRANCOURT

Besides St. Francis de Sales, there was another priority—Général Charles de Gaulle. On the way to visit his home, we went to the village of Blérancourt to visit the National Museum of Franco-American Cooperation. The museum, founded by J.P. Morgan's daughter, commemorates the close ties between France and America since the American Revolution. Wouldn't you know—it was closed! But we strolled through the gorgeous gardens and peeked through the lace-covered windows of the seventeenth-century château that houses documents from Thomas Jefferson, Lafayette, and Benjamin Franklin, as well as art work and a collection of World War I memorabilia. Oh well. Instead, I'll visit the American Friends of Blérancourt in New York.

COLOMBEY LES DEUX ÉGLISES
Général Charles de Gaulle (1890–1970)

"I am a man on whom a great deal of rain has fallen."

Général de Gaulle's ancestors were from an old noble family dating back to the Hundred Years' War when England tried to take France but was defeated by Joan of Arc. During World War II, France was saved again—by Charles de Gaulle.

His father fought in the disastrous Franco-Prussian War. When Paris was starving, he was wounded leading a platoon to forage for food. After the war, he taught philosophy and literature at a Jesuit school in Paris. His mother went to her hometown, Lille, to have her first son. In Paris, three other sons were born.

With his brothers, Charles de Gaulle played with lead soldiers, fighting battles based on Napoleon's victories. As the eldest (and bossiest), he

---

[185] "Capucine," Galerie Bagnoréa, 18 rue Saint Claire, Annecy—Vielle Ville, France.

assigned his brothers their military roles. Xavier was Austria, Jacques was Prussia, and Pierre, Italy. Ten-year-old Charles was, of course, France. With his brothers and cousins, they tramped off to follow Joan of Arc's path from her home in Domrémy[186] through the Loire Valley. At thirteen, Charles de Gaulle was taller than most eighteen-year-olds.

After graduating from St. Cyr Military School, the West Point of France,[187] he joined the infantry under Colonel Philippe Pétain, whom he admired. He named his son after him—the same Pétain who later became a collaborator with Hitler's Nazis and was sentenced to death as a traitor.[188]

During World War I, de Gaulle fought in the trenches, which were "as foul as open sewers." He was wounded by a bayonet, and was left for dead at Verdun after a mine explosion. Miraculously, he survived. He was caught attempting to escape from the hospital and taken as a prisoner of war. He made five escapes from different prisons, where he often slept on straw mattresses full of fleas. In Bavaria,[189] he was sentenced to solitary confinement, but the Germans allowed him to read books that he requested. He perfected his German and trained his memory by memorizing Latin sentences backwards. After nearly three years as a prisoner of war, he was released—a six-foot, five-inch skeleton.

After the war, at an art show in Paris, the thirty-year-old captain met Yvonne Vendroux, who came from a wealthy family in Calais. They were married in 1921 at Nôtre Dame Cathedral in Calais. Both were from very religious, patriotic families. His bride had no idea she had married a "Man of Destiny," but she did know she was an army wife living on army pay in a tiny flat in Paris. During the wild Jazz Era in Paris, with starving artists painting on Montmartre, de Gaulle was assigned to posts in Lebanon, Syria, Palestine, Egypt, Africa, and Turkey. Yvonne followed him from one barracks to another.

As early as 1929, he had predicted war with Germany and wrote a book, *The Army of the Future*, criticizing the army's outdated methods. (They were still using bayonets.) He pleaded for armored tanks with air cover. In France, his book was ignored, but in Germany, it was required

---

[186] In the district of Lorraine.
[187] Eighteen miles from Paris.
[188] The sentence was changed to life imprisonment.
[189] Ingolstadt.

reading for staff officers who copied de Gaulle's exact specifications. In 1933, de Gaulle watched helplessly as Hitler came to power and formed the first panzer division.

In 1939, he and Yvonne bought an old manor house, La Boissérie,[190] in Colombey les Deux Églises, a peaceful, lonely place 126 miles from Paris. He wrote another book, *France and Her Army*, warning against using the Maginot Line of Defense.[191]

Yvonne de Gaulle and Pat Nixon

---

[190] Once used as a brewery, but the town clerk recorded it as La Boissérie.
[191] Named for the French Minister of War, André Maginot (1872–1932), it left the Belgian border open.

When Nazi tanks broke through the Maginot Line, de Gaulle, at forty-nine, was hastily promoted to brigadier général. Général Pétain scorned an offer of union with Great Britain and signed an appeasement with Hitler. He formed a puppet government in Vichy, France, collaborating with the Nazis. De Gaulle flew to England to form the Resistance after being tried in absentia as a traitor and condemned to death by the Vichy government. Winston Churchill's government recognized de Gaulle as head of the Free French Government and helped transport troops to Algeria.

De Gaulle and Daughter Anne

In the meantime, Yvonne and her three children[192] (and a nurse for their daughter, Anne, who had Down's syndrome) left Paris for their home, La Boissérie, where Yvonne received a telegram from London: "Go immediately to the bedside of Aunt Maria." (There was no Aunt Maria. It was their arranged code.) De Gaulle had left her passports and instructions. With her children, a nurse, and two dogs, she left for Brittany. As they were trying to catch the boat from Brest to England, the car broke down. Luggage had to be left behind as they crammed into a borrowed car that arrived just in time to catch the last boat that would be leaving for England for the next four years. The one they had missed was torpedoed and sunk two hours out of the channel. They landed at Falmouth, England, where she read about her husband's broadcast from

---

[192] Philippe, Elizabeth, and Anne.

the night before, calling for French Resistance. When she finally reached him by telephone, he said, "*Voilà*, there you are! Take the next train to London. I shall be waiting at Paddington Station."

Meanwhile, in Paimpol, Brittany, where de Gaulle's mother lived with his brother's daughter, a priest came running to tell them, "I just heard a young French *général* talking from London." He said, "Victory will be ours! The flame of resistance must not die ... Are we going to let them take France like so many tourists?" He was magnificent! De Gaulle's mother grabbed the priest. "Why, that's Charles. That's my son who said that." His mother died a month later. Mountains of flowers covered her grave—the first evidence that anyone had heard him.[193]

In 1943, when Nazi tanks invaded North Africa, de Gaulle flew to Algiers to form the French Committee of National Freedom, which would come to be known as the Provisional Government of the French Republic. "At this very moment, infamous or senile men are trying to hand over our empire to the enemy." In London, his family endured bombing raids day and night during Hitler's Battle for Britain. Prime Minister Churchill was dependent on the United States for aid, and de Gaulle was dependent on Churchill. Although Congress passed a Lend-Lease bill, President Roosevelt, influenced by the State Department, recognized Pétain's Vichy Nazi government. In 1943, when Roosevelt and Churchill met in Casablanca to determine Allied strategy, de Gaulle was not invited. "Where I am, a man must have neither friends nor enemies ... I had to cast myself in ice ..."

He was also excluded from planning the Allied invasion on D-Day. He flew from Africa back to England and boarded a French destroyer for Normandy. (He was on French soil for the first time in four years.) In a British-sponsored broadcast, he called for victory. "I have appointed Caulet commissioner of the French Republic for Normandy. You will obey him in all matters." Now, no one doubted he was their leader. He found General Eisenhower's headquarters in an apple orchard and convinced him of the importance of allowing French Resistance troops to enter Paris, where the Communists were ready to take over the government. General Patton's Tank Corps had been ordered to bypass Paris. The story behind

---

[193] When she died, the Germans censored her obituary notice and made the papers drop the name de Gaulle (which means "of Gaul"). They listed her as Jeanne Maillot, her maiden name.

the victory parade, on August 22, 1944, is a cliffhanger. It is also a miracle. Paris bridges and buildings were ready to be demolished at a signal.

At Gare Montparnasse, German General van Choltitz signed the surrender. With de Gaulle and French Général Leclerc (whose troops had marched 1,800 miles from Africa) was a young naval ensign. When he stiffly saluted, de Gaulle returned the salute smiling into the eyes of his son, Philippe—but the war wasn't over. In December 1944, nineteen thousand GI's were killed in the Battle of the Bulge.[194]

In 1945, when Russian troops took Berlin, de Gaulle flew to Moscow to make a treaty with Stalin against Hitler. To prepare himself for the customary vodka toasts, he drank olive oil to slow the alcohol's absorption. As head of the Provisional Government, he adopted as his personal emblem Joan of Arc's symbol—the double-barred Cross of Lorraine. He united Resistance groups and gave government posts to their leaders, then resigned after two years to form a "Party of the People." He left it in 1953. "It is impossible to work with these people ... I have against me the bourgeoisies, the military, and the diplomats, and for me, only the people who take the métro." He retired to La Boissérie to write his memoirs.

Cross of Lorraine

---

[194] 20,000 were captured and 40,000 wounded.

In 1958, he was called back to cope with a vicious war in Algeria.[195] He agreed to return, but demanded special powers for six months to draft a new constitution. For the first time since Napoleon III, the people would have a direct vote. The following year, he was elected president, and lived at the Élysee in Paris for two terms. As president, he made alliances with former enemies "when their interests become similar to those of France." He withdrew French forces from NATO because France would have no control and had too many other commitments. He also ordered the politically correct bishop of Nôtre Dame not to attend his own church because he had received Pétain, the traitor, there a few months before.

The war for power in Algeria that started in 1954 was between two anti-Gaullist groups—the OAS (Secret Army Organization) and the FLN (Front of Liberation Nationals). Algeria was the capital of the Free French troops, and had been part of France for more than a hundred years. In a televised speech, de Gaulle told his people, "Dear old country. Here we are together again facing a harsh test. Our nation will not permit her unity to be broken. All her children must be strong. All sons and daughters of France will march forward hand in hand ... Once again I call upon Frenchmen wherever they are and whoever they may be to unite France." Even the Communists said, "Nobody has spoken like that since Louis XIV."

Half the army was composed of Communists loyal to Moscow. "We cannot prevent them from being Communists, but we can prevent them from being against France." De Gaulle gave the Algerians, who had been under the Vichy government, the choice of independence. More than one million lived there. "Algerians must determine what they want." They voted for independence. At a conference in Evian, France, he agreed to their decision on the condition that the FLN stop atrocities.

During the next three years, he survived one assassination attempt per year by Algerian anti-independence organizations. One time, bullets punctured two tires. The car skidded when a bullet went through the rear window and hit the frame of a picture of his adored, handicapped daughter, Anne, who had died in 1948. De Gaulle and his wife, Yvonne, got out of the car, brushed the shattered glass off

---

[195] In Oran, more than 3,000 colonists were massacred, mostly French.

their clothes, and de Gaulle said, "They really are bad shots." When a reporter asked Mme. de Gaulle if she was frightened, she replied, "Of what? We would have died together—and no old age."

Another time, out of one hundred shots, twelve struck their car. Both right tires were hit, but, providentially, neither went flat. Their chauffeur kept the car under control, travelling at up to ninety miles an hour. The OAS assassins tried to get between the car and one of the motorcycle escorts. A bodyguard who shielded de Gaulle later discovered that a bullet had pierced his helmet, but had lodged between its sponge rubber linings. One half inch closer, and it would have gone through his head. De Gaulle complimented his wife, "You behaved very well my dear. You were very courageous." She matter-of-factly replied, "Thank you, Charles." In 1968, during a violent student strike, he resigned after the people voted against his program for reorganizing the Senate. He died of a heart attack the next year.

"La Boissérie"

In Colombey les Deux Églises, in the region of Lorraine, an enormous visitor's centre has been built overlooking the plains. Signs all over the place point to "La Boissérie," de Gaulle's modest home in a park-like setting. He and his wife, Yvonne, bought it before Nazi tanks roared in and ruined it. When it was restored, they added a square tower overlooking sweeping fields and distant mountains. De Gaulle used it as a study.

The flower bed in front of the ivy-covered façade is designed in the shape of the Cross of Lorraine. "From one high place in my garden ... I looked where the forest envelopes the place like the sea beating against a promontory ... In a little park, trees are always green. When flowers are planted by my wife, they are soon reborn. Silence fills my house."

Visitors are only allowed into a few downstairs rooms filled with family pictures[196] and gifts from all over the world. La Boissérie is like a shrine—complete silence as tourists quietly trespass on sacred ground.

---

[196] Including de Gaulle's father, who took his children to see Jules Verne's *Around the World in 80 Days* and Edmond Rostand's *Cyrano de Bergerac*.

Only one official foreign guest was ever invited to stay overnight: Konrad Adenauer, Chancellor of West Germany. At La Boissérie, de Gaulle played with his little daughter, Anne—throwing a ball, sailing balloons, singing old French nursery rhymes. When she died at twenty, he told Yvonne, "Now at last our child is like all children."[197] After de Gaulle retired, he and Yvonne enjoyed visits with their son, Philippe, and daughter, Elizabeth, and their children.

During an interview, he told a newspaper reporter, "The Presidency is temporary, but the family is permanent." When asked about President Roosevelt (his nemesis) he charitably remarked, "As he was only human, his willpower cloaked itself in idealism." Regarding his opinion of President Lyndon Johnson, "He was not over-burdened with humility."

In another interview, he said, "The United Nations is an argumental Babel. It is anarchy. If China comes in, it will just add more orators to insult the West." When asked his opinion about the birth control pill in France, "We don't pay for their movies and theatre, so why should we pay for any other entertainment of theirs?"

At the little church he and Yvonne attended every Sunday, we found the place where they knelt between two stained glass windows depicting Joan of Arc and Saint Louis. Outside the church, two marble slabs mark the graves of Général de Gaulle and his daughter Anne, his joy: "... she helped me overcome the failures in all men and to look beyond them." When I asked a lady in the gift shop nearby where his wife, Yvonne, was buried, she was horrified to learn her name wasn't on either tombstone.

On a hill overlooking the beautiful scenic countryside stands an enormous Cross of Lorraine that can be seen for miles. "Someday when I die, I will be buried here, and on this hill, the government may see fit to raise a tall, marble Cross of Lorraine. This is all the memorial I want."

BACK TO PARIS

A visit to France couldn't end without a celebration in Paris. The celebration began with lunch at the famous Le Grand Véfour restaurant,

---

[197] In 1948, in her honor, they founded Foundation Anne de Gaulle, a private hospital for handicapped young girls in Yelines, France.

which started as a coffee stand during the French Revolution. We parked a bright pink backpack on a shelf in the reception area and told the pretty girl at the desk we had come from Texas to see the ashtray modeled after the hand of French writer George Sand—and there it was! Mission accomplished. We were escorted to a cozy corner, a perfect place to view the smooth, choreographed timing of the waiters as they silently glided around the room. The only flaw during the elegant luncheon was when something green got spilled on the spotless, white tablecloth. We tried to hide it under a knife, but the waiter whisked it away for the next course. "Oh dear! He can see it." When we apologized for spoiling the tablecloth, he just raised his eyes to the ceiling and said, "Pigeons."

On the Champs-Élysées,[198] at the Lido, the famous nightclub, we enjoyed more scenic beauty—Gene Kelly's "Dancing in the Rain" number with gorgeous girls in see-through rain coats, plus live animals, ice skaters, acrobats, magicians, and a real waterfall on stage. The elegant, refined show has spectacle, talent, and cuisine that a French chef would call "divine." When you go, make sure you have a ride home. If you find an available taxi afterward, it will be a miracle.

NICE

Besides St. Francis de Sales and de Gaulle, another favorite dead person is Giuseppe Garibaldi. There is a song about the first President of the United States that begins with, "Hail George Washington, man of our need and our destiny fulfillment ..." Both Garibaldi and Washington were men of destiny—destined to free their fellow men from tyranny and unite their countries. Both were admired and respected men of honor. To visit Garibaldi's birthplace, we went to Nice.[199] His huge statue is in the center of Old Town on Garibaldi

---

[198] Named for the Elysian Fields. Marie de Medici turned fields into a long, tree-lined pathway.

[199] His parents' home on the corner of quai Lunel has been demolished. The grounds have been incorporated into the garden of a neighbor's house. The little cottage where he lived with his son, Ricciotti, and helped him with his penmanship (1854, 1856), is still there next to the hospital.

Square, surrounded by fountains. On the beach below Promenade des Anglais, all the nearly-naked sun bathers were lying on pebbles. Opposite the four-mile promenade lined with palm trees, our perfect hotel, Mercure de Fleur, had a shaded patio where two old gentlemen were playing chess at cocktail time. The next morning at breakfast, they were still there, pondering their next move.

For people inclined to get lost, Nice is no problem. Old Town was around the corner from our hotel, down a few streets. The huge sunshiny flower market on Cours Saleya was crowded with people seated at outdoor tables. The Cathedral of Ste. Réparate, patron saint of Nice,[200] is on another popular square—Cours Rossetti.[201] When we arrived, a man was locking the door, but after much pleading and pathetic looks, he let us in to peek at the seventeenth-century Italian baroque interior. The narrow alleys in Old Town are lined with little shops and bistros. One shop owner indicated by pulling on his ears that he was going to string me up by both ears because I had picked up one of his newspapers to read the headlines.

At night, under soft, amber lights, we strolled along Promenade des Anglais, past museums and luxury hotels. At the famous Hotel Negresco,[202] where bellboys wear white gloves and red breeches, we pretended to be rich and famous and walked straight through the lobby into an enormous room, a fabulous private art museum. For me it was old home week—there were so many portraits of people I've always wondered about. The Ladies' Room is inhabited by costumed mannequins. A quick peek at the Men's Room was interrupted by a man in a hurry.

---

[200] A third-century twelve-year-old girl who was martyred.

[201] Named for Garibaldi's journalist friend, Luigi Rossetti, who fought with him in South America.

[202] Named for a Romanian-born hotel man. In 1974, Hotel Negresco was declared a national monument.

PART III

Sardinia and Sicily
with
Guiseppe Garibaldi

7

SARDINIA

Giuseppe Garibaldi (1807–1882)

There is something very attractive in the unassuming simplicity of Garibaldi's character; a total lack of affectation, conceit, or vanity.

—ALFRED, LORD TENNYSON

STILL IN PURSUIT of Garibaldi after visiting friends in France,[203] we left for Rome then flew to Olbia, Sardinia, to visit Garibaldi's home on the island of Caprera. A friendly taxi driver, Angelo, drove us across Sardinia to Palau, where we boarded a ferry to reach the island of La Maddalena. Purple, yellow, and pink flowers,[204] along with strange-shaped colossal rock formations, were everywhere, as well as gorgeous ocean views and luxury resorts. From the port at La Maddelena, a causeway leads to Garibaldi's home. We arrived there the day after the anniversary of Garibaldi's death (June 2, 1882).

---

[203] Paris, Nolay, Lunay, Nîmes, Tarasçon and Marseille.
[204] Bougainvillea, hibiscus, and oleander.

CAPRERA

His white stucco house was larger than I had anticipated. Rooms have been added. In each room, two formidable non-English speakers (male and female) stood on guard. In the last room, an intelligent, personable woman finally spoke English.

We saw the clock (a gift from England) that Garibaldi's son, Manlio, had stopped at the hour Garibaldi died: 6:00 p.m. A calendar still shows the date: June 1882. The kitchen has a large fireplace, water pump, and spit. On display in another room is the bullet taken from Garibaldi's ankle after the battle of Aspromonte in Calabria,[205] along with a picture of his doctor, Dr. Zanetti. Garibaldi's portable bathtub, orthopedic bed, wheelchairs, and canes are also there. Other memorabilia include two leather saddles made in South America, an organ with the original cardboard discs, and candles from the Meucci candle factory, where he worked in New York City. His long white coat, poncho, and famous red shirt are hanging in a bedroom.

Pictures on the walls include his most faithful followers—his devout mother, Rosa, and portraits of his three children by Francesca, his second wife. The most remarkable is a portrait of Garibaldi painted on cloth by his daughter-in-law, Constanza, wife of Ricciotti, Garibaldi's second son by his first wife, Anita. Are you still with me? Garibaldi's deathbed, enclosed by white curtains, is protected on all sides by spiked iron grill work, a gift from the Veteran's Society of Leghorn.

A windmill and a boat given to him by the Sardinian Fleet are in the courtyard near Garibaldi's marble bust. Also, a 138-year-old pine tree—planted the day his daughter, Clelia, was born—grows there. She lived at Caprera until the age of ninety-two. In the cemetery next to Garibaldi's granite tomb—where fresh bouquets of flowers were laid—are the tombs of his second wife, Francesca, and their three children, as well as Garibaldi's daughter, Teresita.[206]

---

[205] There are three different national parks in Calabria. One is Aspromonte.
[206] By his first wife, Anita.

8

SICILY

ERICE AND SEGESTA

OUR GARIBALDI trek had just begun. The next stop was Sicily. To get there, we returned to Rome on a ferry then flew to Palermo. At a restaurant that night, a recording of Frank Sinatra's "New York, New York" welcomed us. This was late on a Sunday, and there were no city tours until Tuesday. The next morning, we booked a tour of two ancient towns, Erice and Segesta. Others on the bus included a few Italians and a group of French people who sang *oo la la's* with our beautiful tour guide when she sang a Sicilian folk song. With no problem, she translated her spiel into four languages.

Erice and Segesta are hilltop towns with spectacular views. The town of Erice leads upward on twisting cobblestone streets to a Norman castle built on the site of a temple to Venus. In a shop carved into the mountainside, we sampled and bought marzipan candy. Centuries ago, when a convent was wiped out in a landslide, the nuns went into business for themselves and made marzipan for sale. One home on the narrow street has a plaque over the balcony dedicated to Garibaldi and his Thousand. The town of Segesta began with the Trojans. A fifth-century theatre dates back to the Carthaginians—from the ancient city-state of Carthage on the African coast. Greek tragedies are still performed here in the summer.

On the tour, we met Mirella from Milan, an education administrator who has visited all the National Parks in the United States. She and her mother were celebrating her mother's birthday. That night we had dinner with them in Palermo and drank a few toasts to her Momma: *a-la Donna* (pronounced *Donnya*).

PALERMO

The Tuesday tour of Palermo (with earphones on top of a bus) was an "on-the-scene" continuing education course in art and architecture. The Phoenicians, who arrived in Palermo more than three thousand years ago from the city-state of Syria, were descendants of Noah's son, Shem. Most of the beautiful churches and buildings have been rebuilt over the centuries. During World War II bombing,[207] many were miraculously spared, including the palace[208] where Garibaldi and Alexandre Dumas had spent two nights. After the bombing, Mother Teresa and her nuns moved into the wealthy Piazza Magione quarter, to the horror of indignant, privileged residents. They resented being told by a Macedonian that "since Palermo is as poor as a Third World Country, charity should begin at home." Her words were effective.

The cathedral is on a site where Phoenicians, Romans, Byzantines, and Arabs had their places of worship. The statue atop a fountain in the Cathedral Piazza is Saint Rosalia, Palermo's patron saint. Rosalia was the niece of twelfth-century Norman King William II, and spent her life in prayer and penance in a cave on Monte Pellegrino overlooking Palermo. Seven hundred years later, in 1624, her remains were discovered.

After we passed the famous three-tiered Fountain of Shame, with its four nude, female figures, the men on the bus were still looking backwards a block away. One of the largest squares in Palermo is Piazza Marina. Garibaldi's Garden, with his monument and busts of

---

[207] In 1943 the port was destroyed, along with many buildings. The Mafia was given funds by the European Union to rebuild the city.

[208] *Palazzo dei Normanni.* Where, on July 22, 1943, the Fascist governor surrendered to the Allies. The entire population cheered, "Down with Mussolini."

the *Risorgimento*[209] leaders, is in the middle of the piazza. At Palermo's picturesque harbor, Garibaldi's men, outnumbered and exhausted, fought and defeated Neapolitan soldiers.

MONREALE

The next day, we found our rental car at the Palermo airport and drove to Monreale, outside Palermo. The guidebook said to "make a beeline" to the cathedral. At the top of a hill, the cathedral dedicated to the Blessed Virgin is the town's main attraction—and knows it. "Queen of the Hill," with houses huddled around its piazza, has the largest icon in the world. Originally for the benefit of illiterate thirteenth-century people (practically everybody), the entire upper half of the interior is covered with colorful mosaics depicting Old and New Testament stories. Twelfth-century Norman King William II commissioned the cathedral to compete with the cathedral in Palermo. Against a glittering gold background, an enormous Byzantine mosaic of the *Pantocrator* (Christ the Ruler of All) dominates the cathedral. You have to pay to see the cloisters, but it's worth it. Two hundred and twenty-eight double columns, decorated with scenes from the Bible, are delicately carved in gold, mosaics, stones, and lava. The view from Monreale is awesome!

SALEMI

From Monreale, we drove a half hour through scenery scattered with fields of red poppies to Salemi, Garibaldi's first halt after landing at Marsala. In Salemi, he announced that he had come in the name of King Victor Emmanuel to free Sicily from Spanish tyranny. The ancient Arab town with narrow streets sprawls over a hill. Next to a seventeenth-century basilica (being restored after an earthquake in 1968),[210] four college girls and one boy were digging in the dirt. They were archeologists from Sweden, Norway, and America.[211] They told us to check at the Civic Museum for Garibaldi information. At the museum, the receptionist—a

---

[209] Movement for the liberation and unification of Italy.
[210] The earthquake left one-third of the population homeless.
[211] Chicago University and Stanford.

girl talking on a cell phone—pointed to a room across the hall. All we saw were remnants of statues and sculptures from destroyed churches.

At the tourist office, Gaspar, a very nice man, went back to the Civic Museum with us and shouted at the girl still talking on the cell phone, who reluctantly walked us upstairs to the Garibaldi Museum, which contains pictures of Garibaldi's officers, newspaper articles, and other memorabilia. Mission accomplished. We had lunch at an outdoor restaurant where the menu included "drinks in a can."

The restaurant window displayed bread shaped as fruit, vegetables, flowers, fish, etc. The bread symbolizes an ancient custom, "Bread for the Poor", that started on the feast day of St. Blaise (*Biagio*), who fled to Sicily from persecution in Armenia.[212] Today the custom is celebrated on St. Joseph's feast day , March 19, with a three- or five-tiered altar of "Bread for the Poor." I wish we had had time to go to nearby Club Bimbo.

GIBELLINA NUOVA

Near Salemi is Gibellina Nuova, where a new town has been built after the 1968 earthquake that demolished the old one. At the town's entrance, a gigantic stone sculpture, *stella* (or "star"), symbolizes the rebirth of the city. Draped across the main street, a lacy decoration with a star in the center resembles a queen's jeweled necklace.

CALATAFIMI

The site of Garibaldi's most famous miracle, his victory at Calatafimi,[213] is eight miles northeast of Salemi. To inquire about a hotel, we parked on a street in front of a statue of Padré Pio, from Pietrelcina,[214] south of Salerno. He was the saint who, like St. Francis of Assisi, suffered the wounds of Christ, the stigmata.[215] A lady told us to go to the cathedral. But where was

---

[212] In Sicily he cured sick animals and healed people with throat problems. When he returned to Armenia, he was martyred. Devotion to St. Blaise was brought to Cleveland, Ohio, by immigrants from Messina.

[213] Another old Arab town.

[214] Today, Pesto.

[215] He received the stigmata on the feast day of St. Francis of Assisi. Father Pio built a hospital on the idea that "Love is the first ingredient in the relief of the suffering." Ex-mayor of New York, Fiorella La Guardia, donated money for a new hospital.

the cathedral? As we drove through narrow streets never meant for cars, we kept passing the same old men lounging in front of a store, and finally found the only hotel in town[216] at the top of a hill around the corner from the cathedral. The guidebook said, "It's a very nice place for a quiet night in the sticks." Ha! Whoever wrote that didn't know the cathedral square is where every teenager in town with a motorcycle congregates until 11:00 p.m. *Mamma Mia*, the owner of our hotel, monitors the curfew. In the twilight, we could see the ridges of a hill in the distance, now covered with grapevines, that Garibaldi's men had to climb under enemy fire.

Calatafimi Hill—"Bixio, here we make Italy or we die."

The next morning, we drove to the top of the hill, where a monument has been erected over the remains of Garibaldi's heroic men who died there. At the end of a shady pathway, an arch is inscribed with Garibaldi's famous words, "Bixio, here we make Italy or we die." Visiting Calatafimi was like finding the Holy Grail.

CEFLAU

On the Tyrrhenian coast, Cefalu (where women run the town[217] and movies are made[218]) is en route to Milazzo. Our hotel was on a hill

---

[216] Hotel Millepini.

[217] Mayor, police chief, unemployment agency, education and entertainment.

[218] Cinema Paradiso.

halfway between the cathedral and a fishing port below. We should have taken the car, but the hotel lady told us, "It was just up the hill." Very funny! It was a half-hour walk straight up a *big* hill, but on our hike we had a spectacular view of the Tyrrhenian coast with rocky beaches. On the opposite side, a gigantic, dramatic-shaped cliff called La Rocca juts into the sky. At night, the lighted rock and cathedral are unforgettable.

The twelfth-century cathedral, dedicated to the Assumption of the Blessed Virgin, resembles a Norman castle. It was built by Norman King Roger II as thanks for safely landing there after a storm at sea. The glorious, mind-boggling Byzantine mosaics of Christ the *Pantocrator*, the Virgin, and Archangels are the oldest mosaics in Sicily.

The hotel lady also told us to go to Castelbuono, on another hill, for a great view. We had a picnic there in front of a weary old church. A young man in his late twenties, who was enjoying the fantastic view during his lunch hour, took our picture. He and his five brothers own a "hydraulic supply" business (plumbing). His name is Roberto, but we rechristened him Bob.

Cefalu is a town of tangled, steep streets. We spent most of the time looking for a bra with plastic straps (no luck), but we did find the house where Garibaldi stayed overnight[219]—thanks to a good-looking teenage boy who was pulling on a rope, sending a bucket of something up to a man on the roof. To make the visit perfect, that night at dinner down by the fishing port, our waiter gave us free lemon cordials, *limoncello*, because we were from America, but he couldn't understand why Americans use phrases like "*pretty* bad."

Another excursion from Cefalu was Gibellmana. At the top of a hill, the lovely and very old church of St. Mary of Gibellmana overlooks the countryside. It stands on a site sacred to the Muslims and is dedicated to the Blessed Virgin.[220] The Capuchin[221] monks have been here since 1535. The white marble altar and statue of Mary and Baby Jesus are the most lifelike you will ever see. We heard the exceptionally melodious church bells that ring every fifteen minutes, but we couldn't visit the town's pride

---

[219] Via La Bolto.

[220] The Koran believes in her Immaculate Conception and her Virgin Birth. It also has verses on the Annunciation, Visitation, and Nativity.

[221] A branch of the Franciscan Order.

and joy—the museum that was once a monastery. A lady told us the priest was taking a nap, and then he would have to shave, so it would be awhile.

MILAZZO

Milazzo, sixty-six miles from Cefalu, is where Ulysses was shipwrecked and where Garibaldi had to take another fort in an all-day bloody battle. A girl at the tourist office told us where to find the Church of Maria Maggiore,[222] where Alexandre Dumas found Garibaldi asleep on the porch. When I asked her how to say, "You make me very happy," she replied with a smile, "*Sol Felici.*" She also told us where to find Garibaldi's headquarters.[223] A Liberty statue on beautiful tree-lined Garibaldi Promenade honors the men who died there during a battle against the Spanish.

Milazzo traffic is scary. All the daredevil drivers should be in the NASCAR races. On the way to Cape Milazzo, clusters of tiny white sailboats floated in the distance on the sparkling blue Tyrrhenian Sea. At the top of a hill overlooking the Cape, you can see the Aeolian Islands.[224] One restaurant was open.[225] The handsome owners, Paolo and Gaetano, decorated our *limoncello* desserts with different designs—one was a Sicilian Valentine heart. *Sol Felici,* guys!

A stairway at the top of Cape Milazzo[226] descends to the rocky sanctuary of St. Anthony of Padua, who found shelter here in January 1221 when his ship was lost in a storm. He was on his way to Morocco to preach after several of his Franciscan brothers had been martyred there. A small church, built in 1575, records the saint's many miracles.

GIARDINI-NAXOX

From Milazzo, we drove to Francavilla di Sicilia in the mountains outside Taormina for the night. We should have been able to see Mount Etna from there, but it was cloudy. The next day, we had fun beach-

---

[222] The end of Garibaldi Promenade by the water (Ancient Maritime Quarter of Vaccarella). The church was dedicated to Jesus and Mary in 1632. Two tablets on the façade commemorate the heroic deeds of Garibaldi and his men on July 20 and 21, 1860.

[223] Palazzo Murchese Proto at Piazza Caio Duilio.

[224] Aeolian Islands named for the Greek God of the Winds, Aeolus.

[225] Giardina Dei Caprici.

[226] Milazzo is surrounded by the sea on three sides.

combing for treasures that we decided must have been washed ashore three thousand years ago. On second thought, maybe the pretty green glass was from a Seven-Up bottle, and maybe the piece of wood wasn't from a sunken ship; maybe it was a shingle off someone's roof.

MESSINA—STRAIT OF MESSINA TO REGGIO CALABRIA

Still trailing Garibaldi, we took off to Messina through mountain tunnels and left our rental car at the Hertz Agency. The car agency is on Via Garibaldi, but since there is no parking place, we left the keys at the office, the car on the street, and waved "bye" (*ciao*).

Although Shakespeare's *Much Ado About Nothing* is set in Messina, he never went there. He must have heard about the traffic. There are two tourist offices in Messina.[227] One has an English speaking person. The other doesn't. We went to the wrong one.

Near the lighthouse in Messina[228] at Faro Point, Garibaldi's men spent three weeks in the August sun on the sand dunes. Messina truly did rise from the ashes like the phoenix. In 1908, an earthquake destroyed ninety percent of the buildings, killing eighty-four thousand people in thirty seconds. During World War II, the Allies (Americans, British, and Canadians) bombed Messina to free people fleeing from the Nazis and Mussolini's Fascists. In 1943, more than twenty-five thousand Allies died during the liberation of Sicily.[229] Statues to Garibaldi, yes. Monuments to the Allies? We didn't see any.

We had bought train tickets to Salerno, Italy. Our ticket was for a train car that had to be ferried across the Strait of Messina to the town of Reggio Calabria in Italy. From there our little train car was hitched to the train to Salerno. On the ferry, if you leave your seat on the train car to go up on deck, bring bread crumbs to find your way back.

---

[227] Via Rizzo.

[228] On the Ionian Coast in the Mediterranean, named for the people of ancient Ionia, near Athens.

[229] Sicily was liberated despite rivalry between American General Patton and the British, who thought the Americans were incompetent. The race to free Palermo and Messina was won by General Patton's Seventh Army. General Patton described himself as "a passenger floating on a river of destiny."

9

ITALY

SALERNO

FROM THE RAILROAD station in Salerno, our hotel was nearby at the end of a beautiful boardwalk with palm trees on one side and the bay on the other. Following Garibaldi's footsteps, Salerno[230] was another overnight stop—where Alexandre Dumas had set off his red, green, and white fireworks, and deliriously happy, liberated people danced in the streets.

After checking into our hotel,[231] we wanted to eat on Corso Garibaldi at a restaurant called Pizza Margherita. Finally, we could have a frozen margarita, but the restaurant was closed. We ate next door on an outdoor patio and learned that Pizza Margherita is a pizza named for Queen Margherita, wife of Naples' Spanish ruler, Uberto (1889). It is the classic combination of tomato sauce and mozzarella cheese, but green basil is added to resemble the colors in the Italian flag.[232] When I asked what *mozzarello di bufalo* meant (I hadn't seen any buffaloes), the waiter patiently explained that there is a mozzarella cheese made from buffalo

---

[230] Where St. Matthew is buried in the cathedral. There was no trace of the bombing during the Allied landing of September 9, 1943, to oust the Nazis.

[231] Jolly Hotel a Lungonare.

[232] Another pizza called Marinara is made without mozzarella. Only tomatoes, garlic, oregano, and olive oil. It is the favorite of sailors from the Marinaro fishing village.

milk, but it's too expensive. Instead, cow's milk is added to goat or sheep milk.[233] When we wanted to know what *Spaghetti alla Puttanesco* means, we were told, "Ladies of the Night." "Oh good. We'll have that."

NAPLES

The train to Naples takes a half hour. In front of the railroad station, no jubilant crowds singing *Garibaldi's Hymn* met us as they did when Garibaldi arrived, but his huge monument is here. From in front of the statue, a bus took us to Castel Buovo, where we boarded another bus for a city tour. The castle, with massive, medieval round towers, is where couples register their weddings. While we waited for the tour to begin, two bridal couples (brides with flowing white gowns dragging in the street) had their pictures taken in front of a double-decker red tour bus. Why? Maybe the *Camorra* (Naples' Mafia) told them to run over there and advertise the Bus Tours.

Wedding Portraits in Naples

From the top deck of the city tour bus, Naples is an outdoor museum. To enjoy all the beauty on foot would take months—if

---

[233] Water buffaloes from India were introduced into southern Italy in the sixteenth century near Salerno. The Nazis destroyed them in 1940, but they are being revived.

you ever get across the streets. Here Garibaldi turned over his conquests to King Victor Emmanuel, freeing the people from merciless tyrants. From the Royal Palace at Piazza Reale, he told wildly cheering crowds, "To this wonderful page in our country's history, another more glorious still will be added. And the slave shall show at last to his free brothers a sharpened sword forged from the links of his fetters ..."

Cathedral of St. Gennaro
(The Duomo)

Naples is almost as old as Rome. The Cathedral of St. Gennaro,[234] dedicated to the Assumption of Our Lady, is named for a third-century bishop born in Naples. He was martyred with six companions, and his chapel in the cathedral is filled with paintings of his miracles.

Behind the high altar, a vial contains St. Gennaro's congealed blood. For the past five hundred years, the blood has liquefied twice a year— on the first Saturday in May, and on September 10. Thousands hold their breath, hoping it will happen again. They believe that if it doesn't, there will be a disaster of some kind! Their soccer team might lose. The cathedral also houses a fourth-century church—the oldest in Naples— built by Emperor Constantine and dedicated to a third-century virgin from Africa, St. Restituta, martyred during the Roman persecutions in Carthage.

Pio Monte Della Misericordia

Around the corner from the cathedral is the Church of Pio Monte della Misericordia, or Church of the Seven Works of Mercy. In 1610, seven young noblemen who were instrumental in promoting city-wide charity built the church. Above the high altar, Caravaggio's most famous painting in Naples depicts the Virgin and Christ Child floating down from heaven into a torch-lit street scene where townspeople are busy carrying out the Seven Acts of Mercy: feed

---

[234] The pagan god, Janus— the god of new beginnings—was given a Christian name, Gennaro. The month of January is named for him.

the hungry, give drink to the thirsty, clothe the naked, visit the sick, shelter the homeless, ransom captives, and bury the dead.

Saint Gregory's Convent
(San Gregorio Armeno)

Saint Gregory's convent is the richest and most important convent in Naples. It was founded in the eighth century by Armenian nuns who escaped persecution in Constantinople. They brought with them the relics of the bishop of Armenia, Saint Gregory. Later, wealthy Neapolitan families bundled their daughters off to the convent to avoid paying dowries.

The Opera House
(Teatro di San Carlo)

The magnificent opera house is the oldest in Europe.[235] Rossini, who composed the opera *The Barber of Seville* (the musical version of Beaumachais' play), was made director of the Teatro di San Carlo in 1815.

Basilica of The Annunciation
(Santissima Annunziata Maggiore)

To the left of the church, a marble doorway leads to a former charitable institution that existed in the early thirteen hundreds to care for unwanted children. Babies were placed on a wheel, and when it was turned, the baby was taken inside the orphanage, where a nun bathed it and recorded the time and date. The former orphanage has been a hospital since the 1980s. Now who cares for abandoned babies?

Mount Vesuvius Funicular (1880–1944)

In 1800, a newly-opened funicular was built to reach the top of Mt. Vesuvius,[236] but everyone was afraid to use it until a song was

---

[235] Opening in 1737.
[236] In an area of Naples (Vomero Hill) near Monte Calvaio in Naples. It stopped running after Vesuvius erupted in 1944.

composed[237] about how romantic it would be. The traditional English version has little relationship to the original but it's fun!

Funiculi, Funicula
(Funicular up, Funicular down)

Some think the world was meant for love and frolic
And so do I, and so do I.
Some think it well to be all melancholy to pine and sigh,
to pine and sigh
But I, I love to spend the hours in singing some joyful song,
some joyful song
To fill the air with music gaily ringing.
Is far from wrong. Is far from wrong.
Harken, harken music sounds afar.
Harken, harken joy is everywhere. Funiculí, Funiculà.

Ste. Lucia

In the 1920's, a Swedish singer on holiday in Naples was intrigued by a song fishermen on the waterfront were singing to encourage people to come for a boat ride. He also noted that streets, restaurants, and hotels were named for Ste. Lucia. He used the fishermen's tune, but changed the words to honor Ste. Lucia.

Santa Lucia

...O'er the calm billows
soft winds are blowing...Here
balmy breezes blow, pure joy invites us
And as we gently row, all things delight us,
Hark how the sailors cry,
joyously echoes high
Santa Lucia, Santa Lucia.

---

[237] It was the first cable car in the world built on an active volcano and was destroyed various times by Vesuvius' eruptions. The funicular stopped running after an eruption in 1944.

In the third century, Ste. Lucia was born in Syracuse, Sicily, to wealthy parents. She became a convert to Christianity during the persecutions of Emperor Diocletian. Although it had been arranged for her to marry a pagan, she had promised herself to remain a virgin. For three years she stalled, in the meantime bringing food and drink to other Christians hiding underground in the dark catacombs. When her pagan fiancé learned she had given her dowry to the poor, he denounced her. Attempts to torture her were miraculously prevented, but eventually her throat was cut. She died December 13, 304 AD.

In Sicily, her name, which means light, is associated with the renewal of faith and hope after dark days of persecution. In 1582, people prayed to her during a famine, and a ship sailed into the harbor loaded with grain. Early missionaries and fishermen brought tales of Ste. Lucia and her miracles to Sweden, which had been converted to Christianity in the thirteenth century. Her devotion spread when, again, during a famine in 1649, a boatload of grain arrived from across Lake Vannern. At the helm, a woman was seen dressed in white with a halo around her head. They believed it was Santa Lucia coming to their rescue.

For more than a thousand years, Sicily and Sweden have celebrated her feast day. In Sweden, December 13th is the longest, darkest day of the year—the winter solstice. Santa Lucia is a symbol of light shining through darkness, bringing light and hope to all mankind. Artists portray her as a blind girl holding a lamp.[238] In the Caribbean, the island Ste. Lucia was named in her honor by French sailors who were shipwrecked and saved on her feast day.

Naples is honeycombed with tunnels, shafts, and underground halls. During World War II, the Nazis bombed entrances to underground tunnels, trapping crowds underneath. American soldiers dug out thousands of desperate people.

The Naples city tour was the best ever because of the beautiful recorded music between stops. After the tour, we went back to the railroad station to pick up the luggage we had checked. For some reason, the railroad agent refused to sell us a ticket on the express train to Rome.

---

[238] She is their patron saint of the blind.

We had to take one that stopped every fifteen minutes as we watched one express train after another whiz by. In the distance we could see the smoking dragon, Mount Vesuvius. A young boy from Lille, France, with his pretty girlfriend, sat near us on the "milk run." I overheard him say, "The taxi drivers tried to kill me! They have no rules!"

ROME

In Rome we stayed overnight at the Marco Polo hotel near the station, but I wish we had known about another hotel in the same building called "Fawlty Towers." Oh well, I would have been disappointed if John Cleese[239] wasn't there. We left Garibaldi on his equestrian monument atop Janiculum Hill and, farther on, Anita's statue galloping full speed on horseback as she cradles a baby in one arm and brandishes a pistol with the other. No wonder Garibaldi was Alexandre Dumas' favorite hero. "If he were to say to me, 'I am setting out tomorrow on an expedition to conquer the moon,' I'd simply reply, 'Good! Drop me a line when you get there!'"

---

[239] An actor who portrayed a hotel owner in the television series, "Fawlty Towers."

PART IV

GARIBALDI'S FREEDOM CAMPAIGNS

1836–1870 ... 34 Years!

10

SOUTH AMERICA

BEFORE HIS DRAMATIC MARCH from Sicily to Naples in 1860 to unite Italy and free people from tyranny, Garibaldi was already world-famous. While under a death penalty for recruiting sailors for the revolutionary leader, Giuseppe Mazzini, Garibaldi escaped to South America to liberate persecuted people there. Argentina and Brazil were both trying to seize the little republic of Rio Grande do Sul in Brazil. "It is the duty of free men ... to fight for the liberty of those who are not free ..."[240]

RIO DE JANEIRO, BRAZIL

In 1836 (the same year as the Battle of the Alamo in Texas) twenty-eight-year-old Garibaldi landed in Rio de Janeiro, Brazil, 5,000 miles from Genoa. He met an Italian journalist, Luigi Rossini, a member of Mazzini's secret organization ("Young Italy"), who introduced him to other members helping the independent republic, Rio Grande do Sul. They helped by sabotaging Brazilian cargo ships. The first ship they captured carried coffee and furniture. Since it was larger, they sank their own ship and sailed away on

---

[240] Garibaldi was born on the 4th of July.

the captured one. When they stopped for supplies and food at a port in Uruguay, officials refused to recognize their Rio Grande do Sul flag. An order went out to seize Garibaldi's ship and arrest the crew. Two ships fired on them, and a bullet hit Garibaldi in the neck. He was kept alive by drinking gallons of coffee. Luckily, they had picked a coffee ship to confiscate.

Eighteen days later, their ship, still intact, landed in Argentina,[241] where a doctor removed the bullet (without anesthesia). Then Garibaldi was arrested. With both wrists bound together, he was tied to a long beam in the roof, dangling four or five feet above the ground. Two hours later, he lost consciousness. When he came to, he was in a prison cell,[242] chained to another prisoner. He was transferred eighty miles to another prison with his arms tied behind his back and his feet tied under a horse. Two months later, he was released and given asylum with the understanding that he would not attempt to escape. His friends, however, rescued him. He arrived in Uruguay with his friend Rossetti. But there, the authorities tried to arrest him again. He and Rossetti hid for a month, then left for Rio Grande do Sul, three hundred miles away.

The coast of Rio Grande was blockaded by the Brazilian navy, and people were starving. The blockade had to be broken. When Garibaldi offered his help, he was made fleet commander. The "fleet" was two old ships in which "every single nail will have to be straightened." With his ridiculous fleet, he went to sea to fight the enemy. He invented his own ingenious tactics and gave the Brazilians endless trouble. No one ever knew where he would turn up.

In 1839 the province of Santa Catherina, north of Rio Grande, also broke away from Brazil and set up a republic. Garibaldi took command of their fleet and freed the port of Laguna, which could then be used as a base against Brazil. One day, as his ship entered the harbor, he saw a beautiful girl through a telescope on deck— eighteen-year-old Anita Ribeiro da Silva, a dark-skinned Brazilian

---

[241] Near Gualaquay.

[242] In Parana.

beauty. When he found her, "We gazed at each other like two people who had met before." In broken Portuguese, he told her, "You must be mine," and off she went to help him fight battles in freezing cold, scorching heat, and days without food or water. Once, when she was pregnant, she was captured and was told that Garibaldi had been killed. She escaped, and after four days on foot and horseback, she found Garibaldi safe in a small village seventy miles away. She survived two fierce sea battles and marched in torrential rain through bamboo jungles with her infant son, Menotti, born in 1840. He, too, lived in the saddle. While crossing mountains in the bitter cold, Garibaldi kept the one-month-old infant in a sling across his chest. "I carried him slung from my neck in a handkerchief." Their baby, Rosita, died of scarlet fever when she was four.[243]

MONTEVIDEO, URUGUAY

For nine years Garibaldi fought in Rio Grande do Sul: three years against Brazil, and six years against Argentina. But after a civil war, disillusioned by treachery and rivalries, he left with Anita and their infant son, Menotti, for Montevideo in Uruguay—again. There was a new government, which made it safe to return. In payment for his services in Rio Grande, Garibaldi was given nine hundred head of cattle. On the fifty-mile trek, six miles inland, most of the cattle were stolen, but Garibaldi finally reached Montevideo penniless. The English foreign minister[244] reported, "His family was living a threadbare existence. He wore a poncho to hide his tattered clothes." He couldn't even afford candles at night. When French Admiral Lainé stopped at Montevideo late at night to deliver an urgent message, he was taken to Garibaldi's shabby cottage, where he gave Garibaldi the dispatch in the dark. When the Admiral was asked what Garibaldi was like, he replied, "I wish I knew. I have talked to him and shaken his hand, but I have never seen him!"

---

[243] "We will see Rosita again, and this life of misery is only an episode of immortality, a divine spark, part of the infinite flame that animates the universe."

[244] Sir William Auseley.

After Argentina destroyed Uruguay's entire fleet, the governor of Uruguay asked Garibaldi for help: "Create me a Navy." With three converted merchant ships, Garibaldi was ordered to sail six hundred miles to attack the Argentine fleet.[245] He sailed away and found their ships after three weeks. For two days and nights, he fought them, then blew up his own ships and disappeared with the survivors.

When the Argentine army headed for Uruguay under the brutal dictator General Rosas, Garibaldi hurried back to defend Montevideo. The siege of Montevideo lasted eight years, but General Rosas never conquered it. In the third year of the siege, Garibaldi was made commander of Uruguay's land and sea forces, and worked with the French and English embassies. He formed his illustrious Italian Legion from the many Italians who had taken refuge there, outfitting them with red shirts that the government had intended for slaughterhouse workers but could not export because of the blockade. His makeshift navy held out until England and France intervened to lift the blockade. When the siege ended, Garibaldi pursued the Argentine army. With his fearless Redshirts, his legion won so many battles that Uruguay's freedom was assured. The battle of Salto-San Antonio, where he was outnumbered six to one, is the most famous. English and French allies were astounded by the "Hero of Montevideo," especially by his scrupulous honesty and humility.

---

[245] An Irishman, Admiral Brown, commanded the Argentine fleet. When he left for Europe after three years in Argentina, he visited Garibaldi to meet him personally. It was a case of mutual admiration.

11

NORTHERN ITALY

FIRST LOMBARDY CAMPAIGN 1848

IN 1848, when thrones were toppling throughout Europe, Garibaldi sent Anita and the children to live with his mother in Nice. Six months later, on a ship provided by Italian exiles in Uruguay, he left for Italy with eighty-three Redshirts and his friend and protector Aguilar, a huge, black Brazilian horse trainer. At a port along the way, he learned about a revolt in Milan where the people had defeated their Austrian rulers and had set up a provisional government.

Garibaldi stopped first at Nice to see Anita, his children, and his mother.[246] He stayed only a few days, then left for Genoa with his volunteers, since he was no longer under a death penalty. The Piedmont constitution had been changed. When he offered his services to the king of Piedmont-Sardinia, the king, Charles Albert, told him to go to Venetia. "They will give you a small ship, and you can ply your trade as a buccaneer. That's your place."

In Milan, Garibaldi was appointed general in the army of Lombardy in northern Italy,[247] but news arrived that the king's troops had been defeated by the Austrians, and the hated rulers had returned. The

---

[246] He hadn't seen his mother in fourteen years.

[247] Lombardy is below Switzerland between the kingdom of Piedmont-Sardinia and Venetia. Milan is the capital.

Milanese were subjected to merciless revenge. Garibaldi was ordered to be captured dead or alive. He escaped with his army to the mountains near Lake Como to fight his own war against the Austrians, using guerilla tactics he had learned from the gauchos in South America. An incredulous Austrian officer said, "They seemed to melt into the earth." Although sick with malaria, he won two battles against thousands of Austrian troops, but the campaign was only a gesture of defiance. On the way through the mountains, he met Mazzini, who carried a banner with the slogan, "God and the People."[248] Mazzini crossed into Switzerland, but Garibaldi marched ten miles south of Lake Maggiore. When he learned that the king had given Austria the regions of Lombardy and Venetia, he issued his famous appeal[249] to the Italian people.

Places en Route to Freedom

---

[248] Mazzini attacked the Communists for being against God, which meant being against morality.

[249] At Castelletto.

... Not able to conform to the humiliating convention which has been signed by the king of Sardinia...my companions and I do not wish to save our lives by infamy and abandon without sacrificing ourselves and our sacred soil to the mockery of those who oppress and ravage it.

The manifesto revived the morale of the Italian army after their defeat. He disbanded his army at Lake Lugano, took a hotel room to recuperate from malaria fever, and eventually returned to Nice and his family.

When Central Italy begged him to free Venice, he led his Redshirts through Florence and over the Apennine mountains. Like Washington's troops at Valley Forge, Garibaldi's volunteers plowed through knee-deep snow, their feet wrapped in rags. At Ravenna, news from Rome changed his plans.

After learning that the Milanese had freed themselves from Austrian tyranny, the people of Rome went berserk. An assassin killed the pope's prime minister, Count Rossi, and a mob stormed the papal palace. Pope Pius IX was terrified and cancelled his previously-instituted reforms. He fled to the port of Gaeta and appealed to Catholic countries to rescue him.

Instead of going to Venice, Garibaldi decided to stay in the Papal States and fight in the Roman revolutionary army. In 1849, the government of the Papal States had been replaced by a republican government. Garibaldi was elected to the newly-formed Constitutional Assembly, but his rheumatism was so painful that he had to be carried into the hall. Mazzini was head of a triumvirate. Garibaldi was to be general, and his volunteers were to be enrolled in the Roman army. Men from all walks of life joined him, including a fifty-year-old priest, Ugo Bassi (one of the most important preachers in Italy), who became their chaplain.

DEFENSE OF THE ROMAN REPUBLIC 1849

Under Pope Piux IX, the new government had passed legislation to reform prisons and insane asylums, grant freedom of the press and religion, mandate secular education, create work for the unemployed, and reduce taxes. However, their policy of lower taxes and increased spending led to inflation and the end of the Republic. The Republic lasted a month. The Austrians defeated King Charles Albert of Piedmont-Sardinia, who had been persuaded to fight for the Roman Republic. He abdicated in favor of his son, Victor Emmanuel,[250] and the victorious Austrians marched toward Rome. "Freedom is a dangerous germ" (Prince Metternich, Austrian foreign minister). To crush the revolt, Spain, France, and the kingdom of Naples sent troops.[251] France, under Emperor Napoleon III, was the first to attack, with more than 2,600 troops. Garibaldi had 1,200 troops, no ammunition, and obsolete, rusty, good-for-nothing flintlocks sent by unscrupulous Count Cavour, the king's prime minister.

Hopelessly outnumbered, Garibaldi's army miraculously defeated the French. Mazzini, however, forbade Garibaldi to pursue them. Instead, a fifteen-day ceasefire was arranged—which was fine with the French, who sent for reinforcements. During the truce, French prisoners were given cigars and a tour of Rome, then allowed to return to their regiments. Not to be outdone in generosity, the French released six hundred Italian nationalists, including Father Ugo Bassi, the legion's chaplain. Impractical Mazzini said, "Let us not make a mortal enemy of France by inflicting a crushing defeat."

In a battle[252] twenty-five miles south of Rome, Garibaldi outwitted the Neapolitans (allies of Austria), but he and his bodyguard, Aguilar, were trampled under the Neapolitan's cavalry. Still recuperating from a bullet wound[253] during the battle, Garibaldi was called back to Rome after the French broke the truce and fortified the hills, including Mount Janiculum, headquarters for the republican army.

After a month of bombardment, Mazzini, who was still in charge, refused to stop the killing. Garibaldi was wounded in his side and lost two of his best friends. One was the gentle giant Aguilar, whom the

---

[250] Victor Emmanuel, king of Piedmont-Sardina, (the constitutional monarch) was short and stout with a ferocious mustache that swept up at the ends. Lady Palmerston, wife of English diplomat Lord Palmerston, commented, "In a fight with a dragon, he would get the best of it."

[251] Ruled by Austria.

[252] At Velletri.

[253] Garibaldi was wounded in the side but waited until dark to call a doctor.

children loved. In the chaos of bombs, bloodshed, and butchery, Anita arrived from Nice on horseback, six months pregnant. Together they went through the last ghastly days of the siege. On June 30, 1849, the Roman Assembly finally agreed to surrender. The United States consul in Rome[254] gave Garibaldi a passport and urged him to come to America. Garibaldi thanked him but refused. "I will not believe that my country's cause is lost ..." In St. Peter's Square, he made his historic speech: "Fortune has betrayed us today, but happier days will come. I am going out from Rome. Those who wish to continue the war may come with me ... Let him come who truly loves his country in his heart and not only with his lips." More than four thousand joined him. A sad, silent crowd watched them go. They cheered only once, when Anita rode up with Father Ugo Bassi by her side. The retreat became as famous as his defense of Rome. The pope and other dictators returned—determined to capture Garibaldi.

FAMOUS RETREAT ACROSS ITALY

For more than a month in the July heat, four armies chased Garibaldi's legion across Italy. The chances of escape were a million to one. From Rome, he marched north across Tuscany and the highest Apennine mountains toward San Marino. For a month, his men forded icy rivers and zigzagged and spiraled through mountain gorges. One enemy commander spluttered, "He's not a general, he's a magician. At this rate, he will lead us to Africa at least!"

The third week, the Austrians captured thirty stragglers. Father Bassi was tortured and shot. Another priest (Father Verita, who over the years had saved the lives of hundreds of patriots) joined them. With the help of an underground guide, the volunteers crossed the Apennines, clinging to cliffs. By the time they made the five-hour descent to reach San Marino, Garibaldi and his legionnaires hadn't slept for three days and nights, and Anita was deathly ill.

At San Marino, Garibaldi told his men they were free to return to their homes. Two hundred stayed, although the Austrians were

---

[254] John David under President Zachary Taylor.

closing in. At the little port of Cesenatico on the Adriatic Sea, they confiscated eleven fishing boats, but there wasn't time to provision them, even with water. Anita was carried aboard with a high fever. Garibaldi wrote, "The moon was fatal to us that night." They were in full view of the Austrians, who sank most of the boats. Garibaldi landed on a little island near Comacchio and waded ashore carrying Anita. His one companion, Captain Culiolo, was still limping from a bullet wound.

In every desperate situation, God sent Garibaldi help. This time, a member of his Roman legion, Giacomo Bonnet (who lived on the island), had seen a convoy of fishing boats and heard gunfire. He guessed it was Garibaldi and ran to the sand dunes where Garibaldi had landed. He was helped by a beachcomber who just happened to be there, and arranged for a boatman to take them off the island. When the man realized his passenger was Garibaldi, he ran away. (The Austrians had threatened death to anyone who aided the fugitives.) Bonnet sent another man with a cart for Anita, who was near death. At a dairy farm in Mandiole near Ravenna, Anita and her unborn baby died.

The underground helped Garibaldi and his lame friend, Captain Culiolo, all the way across Italy. They hid the two fugitives in the bottom of a boat under nets and fishing tackle, and guided them through the forests of Ravenna and across mountains to the kingdom of Piedmont-Sardinia where Garibaldi was arrested and taken to Genoa. He was charged with entering the country illegally. Protests from the free world forced Prime Minister Cavour to issue a statement that Garibaldi had not been arrested, merely detained—"double-speak" used to avoid telling the truth.[255] Garibaldi was released after five days and ordered to leave the country with permission to visit his eighty-year-old mother and his children in Nice for twenty-four hours. His first son, Menotti, was nine, his daughter, Teresita, four, and Ricciotti, another son, two and a half. It was the last time Garibaldi saw his mother.

---

[255] Lord John Russell, British foreign minister wrote, "Cavour can no longer be trusted to tell the truth about anything." (To John Daniel under President Zachary Taylor.)

EXILE—NEW YORK 1850–1853

Dutifully, Garibaldi returned to Genoa, where he was allowed two friends to accompany him into exile; lame Culiolo and Cucelli, the musician from Montevideo who had composed patriotic songs for the Italian Legion to sing on their long voyage[256] back to Italy. But where to go? They stopped for a month at Culiolo's birthplace, La Maddalena, off the coast of Sardinia, and finally found refuge in Tangier, Morocco (eighty miles from Sicily), as guests of the Sardinian consul. Although Garibaldi was in exile again, his body needed a vacation. He wrote his *Memoirs* and stayed seven months, then sailed for Liverpool on a British steamship, then to New York on an American ship. In New York, a wild welcome greeted him,[257] but his rheumatism was so painful he had to be carried ashore "like a bag of hay." All the newspapers carried stories about the world-famous hero of Montevideo and defender of the Roman Republic. He refused press interviews and banquets, and moved out of the old Astor House Hotel to stay with an Italian friend,[258] who gave him a job in his candle factory on Staten Island. When another old friend[259] arrived, he sailed with him on a clipper ship to Lima, Peru, where an Italian merchant gave him command of a ship trading in South and Central Europe and the Far East. Once again back in New York, an Italian captain gave him a ship heading for Newcastle, England to pick up a cargo of coal. He landed at Tynsdale. His five-year exile was over.

LONDON 1854

In London, he was entertained by dukes and duchesses—especially duchesses, who fell in love with the blond, brown-eyed Italian hero with a sultry voice described by one titled lady as "soft,

---

[256] Three months.

[257] 1854 was the same year *Uncle Tom's Cabin* was published. Garibaldi is the only celebrity to ever refuse a ticker tape parade.

[258] Antonio Meucci.

[259] Francesco Carpanetto.

insinuating, with all the authority of a Caesar." Another said, "You only have to look into his face and know this is the one man in the world you would follow blindfolded to death." He became engaged to a wealthy widow, Emma Roberts, but the long, drawn-out dinners with servants standing behind him drove him crazy. He decided, "I don't think so." (They remained friends.)

SECOND LOMBARDY CAMPAIGN 1856

Thinking it would be safe to return to Italy, he left for Nice to see his family.[260] His youngest brother, who worked in Naples for a shipping company, had died and left him some money that he used to buy half an island—Caprera, near Sardinia. On his lonely, rocky island with his fifteen year old son Menotti, and his secretary, Basso, he built a white stone house and tried to stop goats (*capreras*) from eating everything he tried to grow. "At the moment, I am at war with nothing but stones." In 1856, Cavour ordered him to Turin, capital of Piedmont-Sardinia. Cavour said, "Come to see me at daybreak. If I am questioned regarding my relations with you, I shall deny you like Peter and say, 'I know him not'"—the beginning of Cavour's deceitful diplomacy.

To unite northern Italy, Cavour needed Garibaldi's help against Austria, the Papacy, and Ferdinand of Naples, "King of the Two Sicilies" (Sicily and southern Italy). He told Garibaldi that France had agreed to be their ally,[261] but he didn't tell him that France was to get Savoy and Nice in exchange. At the meeting, Garibaldi agreed to fight against Austria for a united Italy in the name of King Victor Emmanuel II, with the understanding that no country must suspect that the king was supporting Garibaldi, Austria's worst enemy.

---

[260] Emma Roberts, his ex-fiancée, and her friend Jessie White, an English nurse, visited Garibaldi in Nice. Emma took Garibaldi's eight-year-old son, Ricciotti, to England, where specialists treated him for a leg problem. She also arranged for his education in Liverpool. Another visitor was Baroness Von Schwartz, a wealthy, tall blond who wanted permission to translate his book into German. He wrote her love letters for two years.

[261] At a secret meeting with French Emperor Napoleon III in Plombières, France, a spa resort west of Colmar.

To get Garibaldi out of the way, Cavour made him a general in the Piedmontese army: second in command, with a gold-braided blue uniform and tricorn[262] plumed hat. Then he sent him to Lombardy again[263] to fight an Austrian army twice the size of his—with, despite promises, no weapons, cavalry, medical supplies, or warm clothes for his men. His troops, however, raided an Austrian barracks and left Milan wearing white linen blouses and jackets. Even his troops were leftovers. "I was kept as a flag to attract volunteers—only those too young or too old or deficient were sent to me. We submitted to all insolence." Before leaving, a friend[264] composed the *Garibaldi Anthem*, their famous battle hymn.

Despite the odds, his Alpine infantry, which included seventeen-year-old Menotti, won battles with their hit-and-run tactics and night marches. At Lake Como, they forced the Austrians back and liberated territory as far as the province of Tyrol in Austria.[265] Garibaldi, wounded in the thigh, conducted the campaign for a month from a carriage and won even more fame.

NAPOLEON III'S SECRET TREATY 1859

In central Italy, French and Piedmontese armies were winning battles, but at Solferino, French Emperor Napoleon III, sickened by the slaughter,[266] made a treaty with twenty-nine-year-old Austrian emperor, Franz Joseph, in which Lombardy went to Piedmont and Austria kept Venetia. That's when Garibaldi learned that Cavour and King Victor Emmanuel had given Nice, his birthplace, to France. "Cavour has made me a foreigner." He told the king, "Now that Nice belongs to France, I am like Jesus Christ. I have no longer a stone on which to lay my head."

---

[262] Three-cornered hat.

[263] He had liberated this territory eleven years before. King Charles Albert gave it back to the Austrians.

[264] Luigi Mercantini.

[265] The capital of the province is Innsbruck.

[266] The French army had only one doctor for five hundred casualties. The suffering on the battlefield led to the founding of the International Red Cross.

It wasn't easy to forgive them—especially Cavour, who had persuaded King Victor Emmanuel to demand Garibaldi's resignation from the Royal Army and exile him to Caprera. As compensation, the king gave him a shotgun. Cavour was terrified Garibaldi would invade the Papal States and take credit for it. Garibaldi issued a proclamation: "I recognize no power on earth as having the right to take away its nationality from an independent people." In Turin he met Alexandre Dumas, who predicted that, within the year, Garibaldi would be the leader of all Italy.

12

SICILY[267]

TWO MESSENGERS FROM Sicily arrived in Turin asking Garibaldi to lead an expedition to Sicily where a revolt had broken out against their despotic Neapolitan rulers. King Victor Emmanuel granted the request, but Prime Minister Cavour demanded that Garibaldi and his volunteers be arrested if they stopped at any port— not, however, if they were on the high seas outside Sardinian waters. Garibaldi's famous Thousand,[268] which included his redshirted Italian Legion from South America, left in two steamships from Quarto, three miles from Genoa, with no supplies—only rusty, useless, muskets[269] to fight twenty-four thousand Neapolitans. Sicily was five thousand miles away. The only one who wasn't seasick was Garibaldi. One man was so seasick he jumped overboard and begged not to be fished out; he would rather drown. When he was rescued, he jumped back into the water.

---

[267] 180 miles long, 120 miles wide. A mountain chain of the Apennines crosses the island.

[268] They were soldiers in name only; most were laborers. The rest were doctors, lawyers, engineers, artists, and businessmen. Ages ranged from twelve to sixty.

[269] Alexandre Dumas wrote that they procured supplies from the governor of a fortress at Orbetello, twelve miles from Talamone. Guns had been obtained by subscription for Garibaldi from all over Europe and America, but Cavour refused to release them.

MARSALA, SALEMI, CALATAFIMI 1860

When they reached the port of Marsala in Sicily, two neutral British warships were in the harbor. Garibaldi was told that the Neapolitan fleet had just left to search for him. If Garibaldi's ships hadn't lost two hours rescuing the suicidal, seasick man, his ships would have run straight into the enemy. After landing at Marsala, Garibaldi's men scuttled their ships and seized the telegraph office to cut the wires. When they were safely inside the walls (entering from today's Garibaldi Gate), the Neapolitan ships returned, their commanders puzzled by British ships in the harbor. They hadn't been there before. England helped again when he crossed the Strait of Messina.

Garibaldi addressed the Marsala Town Council and told them that everything he did would be in the name of King Victor Emmanuel. "I have brought you a handful of brave men ... We seek nothing but the liberation of Italy ..." The next morning, the Thousand, led by Garibaldi in his red shirt, marched to the mountain pass of Salemi.[270] With him were more volunteers and a new chaplain (in his red shirt), Father John Pantaleo, a quiet, scholarly philosophy teacher. Thomas Nast, the American artist-cartoonist,[271] was also there—armed with a cheese knife.

During the first battle at Calatafimi (where we had encountered the motorcycle kids), the enemy was entrenched at the top of the steep hill, and Garibaldi's men had to fight their way up ridge by ridge with no ammunition—only bayonets. Near the last ridge, a hail of stones crashed down on them. Instead of accepting certain death, Garibaldi shouted, "They are out of ammunition" and charged to the top with his men behind him. When the Neapolitans saw the Redshirts rushing toward them, they fled, throwing down their arms. Actually, the enemy was not out of ammunition. One hundred ten Redshirts were killed or wounded. One bullet hit Garibaldi's son, Menotti, in the hand. After a day's rest, they stopped at a church in the town of Alcamo, where Father Pantaleo gave Garibaldi his blessing in the name of God, Italy, and Liberty.

---

[270] At Salemi, Garibaldi proclaimed himself dictator in the name of King Victor Emmanuel.

[271] The first to draw Santa Claus as we know him today, inspired by Clement Moore's poem, *The Night Before Christmas*.

PALERMO

On the way to Palermo, people fell on their knees thanking the liberation army. Garibaldi's decision to reach Palermo by way of Parco would have been an insane idea from anyone but Garibaldi. His men had to cross the top of three mountains. To deceive the Neapolitans, the *Picciotti* (Sicilian volunteers)[272] kept fires burning on different hilltops every night. Although Neapolitan commanders had no idea where Garibaldi was, a London reporter[273] for the *Times* found Garibaldi's men in "what seemed to be a gypsy camp with horses tethered beneath olive trees, cloaks spread out among the boulders, and everyone gathered around a campfire cooking an ox in a kettle." The bearded survivors of Calatifimi, in rags, with their boots falling apart and faces black from gunpowder, had climbed, crawled, and marched for six days through heavy rain, scorching sun, and cold nights, without food or sleep. They were in the wildest terrain since South America. On the seventh day, they rested on top of a mountain at Parco, overlooking Palermo, which was defended by a force twenty times as large as theirs. Their only hope was a surprise attack.

Garibaldi had led his men up the only route left open—straight up a cliff. Local guides appeared out of nowhere to lead them across the country. To fool enemy spies, he had marched his men in a wide half-circle back to where they had started. He also sent a column along a highway leading to the interior of the island. Spies saw them go and set out after them, but at night Garibaldi changed direction. The next day, his main army attacked while the enemy was still chasing the decoy column. Only seven hundred and fifty of the original Thousand remained. His three thousand volunteers were untrained Sicilians with pickaxes.[274]

On May 26, his army descended the mountain into groves of lemon and orange trees. After three days of fierce fighting, the enemy fell

---

[272] Ninety percent were illiterate.

[273] Colonel Ebner.

[274] Desperate for ammunition, scientists with Garibaldi set up their equipment in the middle of the street to make gunpowder.

back behind the walls of the fortress. They discovered, too late, that Garibaldi was behind them, not in front. When Neapolitan General von Mechel returned with reinforcements after chasing Garibaldi's elusive column, General Lanza, commander of the Neapolitan fort, had already sued for an armistice. "If von Mechel had returned one day earlier, we should have been lost." During truce negotiations, a Greek ship arrived with a cargo of powder for Garibaldi. When Naples' King Francis II signed a formal surrender, twenty thousand soldiers filed out of the fortress, laid down twenty thousand guns, and left all their cannons. Steamers from Naples arrived to take the troops away. They had surrendered to a small, ragged army with rusty muskets and no ammunition or cavalry.

Alexandre Dumas, with seven companions, arrived in Palermo and occupied eighteen rooms on the first floor of the Royal Palace. Garibaldi stayed in a little pavilion at the end of a terrace. Dumas wrote, "We have had a band play to us twice daily. There are two bands. When one finishes, the other starts under Garibaldi's windows and mine. As soon as the Garibaldi band has played its program, it comes and plays beneath my windows, while my band goes away to play under Garibaldi's." He also noted that everyone wanted to wear red. The price of red material doubled. "As a result, all the streets and public places in Palermo give one the impression of being in a vast field of poppies."

MILAZZO

Before Garibaldi could reach southern Italy, he had to cross the Strait of Messina, which was guarded by enemy fortresses. One, at the Cape of Milazzo, was surrounded on three sides by the sea. The only approach was through fields of prickly pear trees and sugar cane so high the two armies couldn't see each other. For eight hours, on shore and in the streets of Milazzo, Garibaldi's volunteers fought a bloody battle in the July heat.

Garibaldi arrived from Palermo with more volunteers (sailing on an old Scottish cattle boat, the *City of Aberdeen)* to take command.[275]

---

[275] Alexandre Dumas followed the army in two carriages with his entourage.

Again, against all odds, Neapolitan troops retreated behind their fortress walls. Help came when another ship arrived with ten guns. It was the rickety Neapolitan paddle steamer, the *Türköry*, that had deserted to Garibaldi in Palermo. Garibaldi rowed out to the ship and climbed the mast to look over the whole field. As he rowed toward the *Türköry*, cannonballs fired from the fort should have sunk him and the steamer, but the marksmanship was so bad that the cannonballs whistled past and fell into the sea. Garibaldi sailed around the fortress close enough to bomb the soldiers guarding the shore, then they, too, ran behind the ring of fortifications.

Now Garibaldi had to take the fort on the hill. Here, the enemy was out of food. Five thousand half-starved Neapolitan troops marched out, leaving horses, cannons, and ammunition. Ships from Naples arrived to evacuate them. When Alexandre Dumas arrived in Milazzo, he found Garibaldi and his staff asleep on the stone porch of St. Maria Maggiori's church, near the water.

STRAIT OF MESSINA

There remained one more fortress in Sicily: the strongest of all, at Messina. However, after hearing that the fort at Milazzo had fallen, the commander only growled, "Where do I sign?" Fifty-five hundred Neapolitans gave up without a fight. Cavour was furious and criticized the Neapolitans for their cowardly surrender that allowed Garibaldi his freedom. "If he crosses to the mainland, he will be the entire master of the situation. Hold him back on any pretext whatsoever." Poor Cavour. He was so devious and cynical, he couldn't believe there was such a thing as an honorable man. He had never met a Garibaldi.

Now to cross to southern Italy, [276] part of Two Sicilies held by Francis II, king of Naples. Garibaldi's volunteers spent three weeks in August on the sand dunes of Messina's Faro Point near the lighthouse. While keeping the enemy's attention on the Faro camp, a second force from Palermo had been secretly gathering thirty miles

---

[276] A British steamer, the *Queen of England*, had brought him twenty-three thousand Enfield rifles.

to the south, where two of his ships had landed undetected.[277] When Garibaldi arrived, the men were already on board. Garibaldi took one ship, and his friend Bixio followed in the other. At night they crossed the narrowest part of the strait[278] and landed twelve miles south of Reggio in Italy, where they met the first group that had been blown off course. They were joined by more than four thousand local volunteers. The main army was still stranded on the sand dunes.

---

[277] Garibaldi plugged a leak in the *Franklin* with manure.
[278] The Straits of Messina are twenty-four miles long, and two-to-four miles in width.

13

SOUTHERN ITALY

REGGIO

PART OF GARIBALDI'S Thousand was now on the mainland. Their next objective was the fortress at Reggio. Fortunately, people fed them along the way with wine, bread, melons, and grapes. They hadn't eaten in three days. At Reggio, again, they were behind the unsuspecting enemy's fortress, where all the guns pointed toward the sea. At midnight they attacked, and by dawn they held the town. The elderly commander of the fortress suddenly found the hills above the town covered with Redshirts. He surrendered but was very indignant: "I expected Garibaldi to attack me in front. Instead, he came from behind."

While Reggio was being attacked, an alarm had sounded at Messina, and the whole Neapolitan fleet had steamed south, leaving the strait unguarded. Garibaldi's main army, still on shore by the lighthouse and still deceiving the enemy, rowed safely across to the mainland to attack two more forts.[279] At the first one, four men approached waving a flag of truce. They said they couldn't surrender because they didn't have orders from Naples. Garibaldi told them, "You never will receive them. I have cut off every line

---

[279] 168 boats, twenty-two men in each.

179

of communication." They were terrified! Nearly nine thousand fled. When Garibaldi caught up with them, he asked, "Why do you flee from us? We are sons of Italy, and so are you ... You are at liberty. Whoever wishes may go home." Instead, many joined him. The next day, the remaining three forts guarding the strait opened their gates.

MOP-UP OPERATIONS IN SALERNO AND NAPLES

Then began the march up the peninsula from Reggio to Salerno. Garibaldi traveled with six others ahead of his army—through mountains, forests, and valleys—on horseback and mules. Since landing on the mainland, his volunteers had walked 120 miles in twelve days. Accompanying them were English journalists, Alexandre Dumas' entourage, and red-headed nurse Jessie White Mario,[280] who cared for the wounded and set up field hospitals with the help of Sicilian women.

From Reggio to Naples there were no more battles. When they reached Salerno, they discovered that the Neapolitan army had left the day before, and King Francis II[281] had fled north of Naples to Gaeta. Upon Garibaldi's arrival, twenty thousand people cheered, sang, and danced in the street. Dumas, who had brought fireworks with him, lit the sky with Italy's colors: red, green, and white. Garibaldi boarded a train to Naples with the American artist Thomas Nash and a few others. It was only thirty-five miles away, but progress was slow: cheering people blocked the tracks.

In Naples he was greeted by a frenzied, yelling mob. Crowds clung to his carriage like swarming bees. When a man fell down in the street, an English tourist concluded the man was drunk. His landlady informed him, "No. It is for joy. You English who have always been free, you cannot imagine the joy of deliverance."

On the way to the cathedral[282] in an open, flag-draped carriage, Garibaldi drove past the cannons of a fortress, but no shots were

---

[280] She married an Italian friend of Garibaldi's.
[281] King Ferdinand died in 1859, succeeded by his son, Francis II.
[282] St. Janarius.

fired. At the cathedral, Father Pantaleo, the Sicilian chaplain, celebrated a Mass of Thanksgiving. From a balcony, Garibaldi told the crowd that he was not fighting against God but against tyranny and papal power. "It is a solemn day when people pass from the yoke of servitude to the rank of a free nation ... Make yourselves worthy of it by stretching out a helping hand in your turn to those who are still suffering and in bondage."

Garibaldi was politically naive. Naples was the most corrupt city in Europe. "The union with Naples was like going to bed with someone suffering from smallpox." Jealous of Garibaldi's popularity and afraid Garibaldi would become dictator of Naples and Sicily, Cavour sent agents to undermine Garibaldi's provisional government. He also paid two Neapolitans to murder Garibaldi: "He might have to be halted at the point of a gun." During Garibaldi's two-month dictatorship,[283] during which he ordered land reforms, unemployment relief, etc., the wealthy, privileged people hated him—especially when he appointed Alexandre Dumas, a foreigner, as Director of Ancient Monuments. Mostly, they feared the Redshirts, who interrupted the opera and demanded that the orchestra play the *Garibaldi Anthem*, "Two seas and the Alps shall our Italy bound; the oppressor no more in our land shall be found ..." Garibaldi's army was headquartered in a palace at Caserta near Naples—the largest in Europe, another Versailles only bigger. Garibaldi moved into one of the smaller rooms. "We occupied the nest while it was still warm."

PAPAL STATES
(The Battle of Volturna vs Neopolitan King Francis II)

While Garibaldi was coping with the evil government in Naples, King Victor Emmanuel's army took the two remaining Papal States[284] and imposed Piedmont's anti-clerical laws.[285] Meanwhile, there was

---

[283] Always in the name of Victor Emmanuel.

[284] Umbria and Marches.

[285] Bishops were imprisoned and church property seized. More than twenty thousand nuns, monks, and friars were dispossessed. In Florence, fifty-three convents closed; they were the refuge and employment for girls whose families could not afford dowries.

still Neapolitan King Francis II, with his fifty thousand French and Austrian allies, behind the Volturna River at Gaeta. The Battle of Volturna was the closest battle Garibaldi ever fought, and the first defensive one. But his angels were still on duty. Fog settled over the battlefield, and the enemy made the mistake of dividing their forces. An entire column lost its way in the fog. When two thousand enemy troops disobeyed an order to retreat, Garibaldi's Redshirts surrounded them. Reinforcements for Garibaldi arrived the next day, and King Francis's Neapolitan troops surrendered. King Victor Emmanuel II, after defeating the Papal army, crossed the Neapolitan frontier with his troops and issued a proclamation that he was taking possession of his Neapolitan province.

DISMISSAL

On a cold October day, Garibaldi and a few officers met King Victor Emmanuel and his Royal Army at a crossroad thirty miles north of Naples. As the pompous procession approached, with glittering uniforms, bands blaring, and banners waving, the disdainful royal troops acted as if they were the liberators of Italy. On horseback, wrapped in his poncho, Garibaldi doffed his hat to his king and said, "I salute the first king of Italy."

How are you dear Garibaldi?
I am well your majesty, and you?
Fine, Fine. They rode on together.
What is the state of your troops?
Very tired, Sire.
That is not surprising considering how long they have fought.
My own troops are quite fresh. Yours can rest.

Garibaldi knew Cavour had coached the king. It meant, "You are no longer needed." A few days later, the king was to review Garibaldi's volunteers. The proud army that had won ten battles to unite Italy stood at attention for hours. The king never showed up.

On November 7, 1860, King Victor Emmanuel made his triumphal entry into Naples, with Garibaldi beside him in an open carriage, during a thunderstorm. Italy was now one free nation from the Alps to the sea, except for Venice and Rome. At the royal palace during the celebration ceremonies, there was no mention of Garibaldi or his Thousand. Privately, the king offered Garibaldi a title, a castle, a yacht, and rewards for his children. Garibaldi politely refused. He told the king he could not be bought with material rewards. He had asked only one thing, that his troops be included in the Royal Army. His one request was denied. (He was told that as volunteers, they did not qualify as regular enlisted soldiers.) Garibaldi left Naples[286] for Caprera with his son, Menotti, his secretary, Basso, and Coltelletti, one of the famous Thousand. He accepted a bag of coffee, fried beans, a sack of dried fish, and a case of macaroni.

BACK TO CAPRERA 1860

Indignation and sympathy poured in from around the world—tons of mail and presents, including two black stallions from the Egyptian pasha and chairs engraved with the names of United States officers. So many sightseers came on yachts that a hotel was built on the island of La Maddalena, a half mile from Caprera. Some of his famous Thousand Redshirts camped outdoors on the island and cooked fish over campfires. Garibaldi's sixteen-year-old daughter, Teresita, was hostess. Both she and Garibaldi sang old gaucho songs and songs from Verdi and Rossini's operas.

"INVITED" TO TURIN AGAIN 1861

Prime Minister Cavour died June 5, 1861.[287] French Emperor Louis Napoleon III worried, "whether without the coachman, the horses may bolt and refuse to re-enter their stable." In the middle of winter, the king and the new prime minister[288] called Garibaldi

---

[286] On the *Washington*, a steamer owned by Captain William de Rohan from Philadelphia.

[287] A local parish priest who had been expelled by the government gave him last rites, despite no confession from Cavour. The priest was suspended by the pope and died destitute.

[288] Urbano Rattazzi.

to Turin, where Garibaldi agreed not to invade the Tyrol. However, some of his men disagreed and started to march. They were arrested and imprisoned. Protests and demonstrations against the Italian government were so violent that in order to placate Garibaldi, the prime minister led him to believe that if he did invade the Tyrol or the Papal States, the government would back him.

BACK TO SICILY 1861–1862
Battle at Aspromonte

He stayed at Caprera for ten days, then left for Sicily, where the governor was an old friend and colleague.[289] As Garibaldi traveled throughout Sicily, urging Sicilians to march on Rome,[290] the embarrassed governor resigned. His successor, General Cugia, did nothing to stop Garibaldi. When orders arrived from King Victor Emmanuel to prevent Garibaldi's legion from entering the harbor of Catania, it was too late; Garibaldi's troops had already landed and crossed the strait into Italy. However, in the wild, isolated mountains of Aspromonte in Calabria, the king's troops attacked and defeated Garibaldi's volunteer army. Garibaldi's conscience wouldn't let him kill his own countrymen. Austrians, the oppressors, yes, but not his fellow Italians. Both he and Menotti were wounded—Menotti in the leg and Garibaldi below the ankle. It took fifteen hours to get them down the mountain on stretchers. Instead of being treated at a nearby hospital, they were taken[291] forty-three miles to Scilla on an Italian ship and kept on board twenty-four hours—Garibaldi in horrible pain—before being transferred to a fortress in Varignano.[292] British and American sea-captains sent medical supplies, and twelve doctors arrived from Italy, Great Britain, and Germany. British Lady Palmerston sent a special bed. With eight officers, Garibaldi and Menotti were held prisoner from August 29 until October 22. After

---

[289] Colonel Pallavincino.
[290] Today the region is divided between the Austrian state of Tyrol and the Italian provinces of Tyrol and Trentino.
[291] With eight officers.
[292] Near Spezia above Leghorn.

Garibaldi had been examined for three months by surgeons from different countries, an Italian doctor[293] finally removed the bullet from beneath the ankle bone in Garibaldi's left foot.

"BACK TO CAPRERA"

In December, Garibaldi went "back to Caprera"—which should be the title of his autobiography. Again, there was worldwide sympathy to compensate for the callous treatment by the Italian government. Baroness von Schwartz visited again and stayed in the guest room at Caprera.[294] She said it had one chair, a table, a hard bed, and cows stared at her through the window. All the cows had names. The donkeys were named for Garibaldi's enemies. One English lady who visited Caprera found a man digging potatoes wearing a strange uniform: Garibaldi's general's uniform.

RETURN TO ENGLAND 1864

After recuperating for a year, Garibaldi returned to England, still using a cane. A French journalist predicted he would get plenty of plum pudding, turtle soup, and sandwiches, but no money for muskets. Both his sons accompanied him, along with his doctor and two secretaries. For eight days, he stayed on the Isle of Wight as the guest of a wealthy Liberal. He also met two admirers: the poet Alfred, Lord Tennyson and Florence Nightingale. In London, the streets were lined with banners reading, "Welcome to the Hero of Italy," while bands and barrel organs played the *Garibaldi Anthem.* Shops closed for three days. They even named Garibaldi Biscuits for him.

During a reception at the new Crystal Palace four miles outside London, thirty thousand people came to honor him. He stayed with the Duke and Duchess of Sutherland and attended banquets and receptions for two weeks. Queen Victoria's son, the Prince of

---

[293] Dr. Zanetti.

[294] In the library she noticed books by Plutarch, Sir Walter Scott, La Fontaine, books of poetry, and Greek and Roman history.

Wales (the future King Edward VII), who had met Garibaldi, told his mother, "He is not tall but has such a dignified and noble appearance and such a quiet and gentle way of speaking, especially, never of himself, that nobody who sees him cannot fail to be attracted by him ..." The queen had a different opinion. She regretted that government officials should have lavished honors usually reserved for royalty. Her daughter, Victoria, disagreed: "I have a secret weakness for that individual. I feel much interest in what he is about."

While the "Hero of Two Worlds" was being fêted as the darling of high society, his sons and friends were ignored. After two exhausting weeks, the Duke and Duchess of Sutherland brought Garibaldi "back to Caprera" on their yacht, and—surprise!—some of his English friends had bought the southern half of Caprera for him.

BACK TO ITALY
Third Lombardy Campaign 1866

Caprera was not a happy place, "Nailed here by my dreadful rheumatism." He also suffered from the ankle wound that had opened, but when King Victor Emmanuel wanted Garibaldi for a third campaign against Austria in the Tyrolean mountains, he obeyed. He left with his Redshirts and his two sons, with no equipment and useless muskets—again betrayed, a word that hurts in any language. When Victor Emmanuel's Italian troops fled, Garibaldi, at Trento, was ordered to halt the campaign against Austria. Prussia, Italy's ally, had defeated the Austrians in Bohemia.[295] At the Treaty of Vienna, Prussia gave Venetia to the French, who had promised to stay neutral. One week later Napoleon III gave Venetia to Italy in exchange for Italy not interfering during the annexation of Savoy and Nice. Garibaldi could now visit Venice with his daughter, Teresita, and her husband.

---

[295] Battle of Sadowa, July 3, 1866.

Giuseppe Garibaldi
Portrait Painted on Cloth by Constanz, Wife of Son Ricciotti

VENICE

Crowds cheering Garibaldi packed the palazzos, and gondolas jammed the canals. Garibaldi reminded the Venetians that only Rome remained outside a united Italy: "Rome is ours and ours legally, so we can go to Rome as we can go into a room of our own house." In Verona, too, he called for a march on Rome, which made foreign powers very nervous. When the Italian government issued a proclamation that the frontiers of a foreign state must not be violated, he decided that that was just another go-ahead signal, meaning that, ostensibly, the government would not be responsible—the usual underhanded game. He told everyone he was on his way to Rome.

MARCHES ON ROME 1867 AND ESCAPES
Second and Third Time

Outside Orvieto, he was arrested in bed before dawn and taken on a train as prisoner to Alessandria, near Turin.[296] Again, there was such an uproar that he was released, put on a ship at Genoa, and sent "back to Caprera." The government ordered nine warships to patrol the island to make sure he didn't escape, but he did! He dyed his beard black and had a friend impersonate him walking around Caprera on crutches. At midnight in a God-sent fog, he muffled a boat's oars and rowed across the narrow strip of water between Caprera and the island of La Maddalena where he met a friend from South American days[297] who was living there. His friend rode horseback with him across La Maddalena to the opposite side of the island where they met Garibaldi's secretary, Basso, and Captain Cuneo, one of the Thousand.

That night a fishing boat took the three fugitives to the east coast of Sardinia. For seventeen hours they rode horseback nonstop across Sardinia's rough mountains to the port of San Palo. After recuperating at another friend's house, they sailed for Italy[298] in a boat arranged by his daughter Teresita's husband. They landed near Leghorn and hired two carriages. Seventy-three miles later, the escape artist popped up in Florence. Garibaldi was particularly proud of that escape.

The next day he left Florence for the Papal frontier where, in cornfields and behind hay stacks, he defeated the Papal troops at Monte Rotando. But when the French sent soldiers from Toulon, and King Victor Emmanuel sent the Italian army against him, Garibaldi surrendered at Mentana and escaped by train. At Perugia,[299] he was hauled off the train and taken to Varignano, the same fortress where he had been held after his capture in the mountains of Aspromonte. Thanks to United States Minister John Daniel, he was released after three weeks and sent "back to Caprera."

---

[296] His men were either arrested or deported. Nurse Jessie White Mario brought him his portable bathtub that he had to leave behind.

[297] Major Susini.

[298] Two and a half days.

[299] Eighty-five miles north of Rome.

VICTOR EMMANUEL TAKES ROME 1870

When Prussia invaded France in 1870, Emperor Louis Napoleon III withdrew his French troops from Rome; three weeks later, the Italian army moved in. Garibaldi's dream of a united Italy had come true, although the "Roman Question" wasn't settled until sixty years and four popes later. The popes preferred to be prisoners in the Vatican rather than accept a treaty giving them certain rights and privileges; they knew that a new government could repeal the Guarantee Laws and evict them. In 1929, Pope Pius XI signed a treaty with Benito Mussolini. One of the compromises stated that girls who belonged to the Fascist Youth Group would no longer be required to carry guns in parades—only bows and arrows.

FRANCE 1870–1871
Garibaldi Commands Army of Vosges against Prussia and Escapes

When King Victor Emmanuel took Rome, Garibaldi was in France, helping his old enemy fight Bismarck's militant imperialism. "I cannot endure to see her crushed." He was sixty-four, stiff with arthritis, and lame from old sword and bullet wounds. Nevertheless, "I offer what is left of me to the service of France against the world." A French doctor, Bordonne, who had been with him in Sicily and Naples, had cabled him to come to France. Garibaldi answered, "My dear Bordonne, if I can get out of my prison (Caprera), I will be with you." One day Bordonne showed up at Caprera[300] and announced, "Well, General, here I am!" and off they went to France with Basso, the secretary, and Garibaldi's two sons.

In Tours, the temporary capital while Paris was being bombed by the Prussians, Garibaldi was given command of the Army of the Vosges, a mountain range along the Rhine. Again, his twenty thousand volunteers from all nations were not considered part of the regular army. Headquarters were at Dôle (where Louis Pasteur was born), but the fighting was mostly around Dijon. Sixty-year-old, white-bearded Garibaldi often traveled with

---

[300] Via Bonifacio and Corsica.

Auguste Bartholdi, who later designed and built the Statue of Liberty. They traveled together inspecting troops and rounding up supplies. That winter, fighting in deep snow, they suffered terribly—especially Garibaldi, who was in constant pain from rheumatism.

On January 21, in zero-degree weather, the Germans attacked Dijon. After a three-day battle, they retreated. It was an incredible victory, and Garibaldi was elected to the French National Assembly. Later, Prussian General Manteuffel said, "There is only one Garibaldi. He is still a unique military genius."

When Garibaldi appeared at the Assembly in Bordeaux,[301] there was so much animosity toward "the outsider" that he was shouted down and not allowed to speak. The same thing happened to Victor Hugo when he reminded the French National Assembly that "None of the powers of Europe came to our aid, but one man came, the heroic Garibaldi ... He is the only one of the generals fighting for France who was not beaten."[302]

"BACK TO CAPRERA"

When Paris fell to Prussia, Garibaldi was still fighting along frozen roads. With his sons, he escaped to Marseille and headed "back to Caprera." Once "back to Caprera" he married Francesca, the mother of three of his six children. He worked with self-help agencies, encouraging the people to stop "bowing and scraping." He told the wealthy their main duty was to improve the conditions of the poor. His arthritis became so bad that eventually he was confined to a wheelchair, and later to this bed. By now, the Busy Body was exhausted trying to follow him. He died at seventy-four, June 2, 1882, in his four-poster iron bed where he could see a picture of his mother on the wall. "I am not a superstitious man, but often when I have passed unharmed through the breakers of the ocean or the tumult of battle, my mother has seemed present with me like a guardian angel."

---

[301] The government had fled to Bordeaux as the Germans advanced toward Tours.

[302] Garibaldi won battles at Chatillon, Autun, and Dijon. His son Ricciotti attacked more than eight hundred Germans at Châatillon-sur-Loire and captured their regimental flag.

ABOUT THE AUTHOR

MARY JANE WILSON is a well-known speaker for conventions and professional groups in and out of Dallas. A graduate of Skidmore College, she has taught speech at Ursuline Academy, and has been featured in a variety of movies and television commercials with the Kim Dawson Agency.

This is her third Busy Body Book. The first book, *Europe with a Busy Body*, includes Germany, Italy, and Austria. The second book, *Back to Europe with the Busy Body*, includes France, Luxembourg, Belgium, The Hague, Holland, Poland, and Greece.

The Dallas actress mixes history and travel advice in a well-researched book. She finds the amusing anecdote or telling feature to make historical personalities come alive.

The Dallas Morning News

CONTACT

www.waldobrucepublishing.com
Email: waldobrucepublishing@yahoo.com

PLACES OF INTEREST

THE BASQUE COUNTRY

SANTIAGO DE COMPOSTELA

Museum
Museo das Peregrina; pilgrimage display and medieval town life.

Tourist Office
Rua do Vilar 63

Hotels and Restaurants

Hotel Costa Vella
Porta da Pena 17—wonderful views.

Hotel Parador
Five-star hotel—Plaza do Obradoiro; oldest in the world. Once a fifteenth-century pilgrim hospital.

Café Literario Praza
Quintan 1—an attractive and unusual square with terrace.
Tel: 981.565.630

Casa Marcelo
Most picturesque restaurant, Rua des St. Hortas.
Tel. 981.558.850

Marte Av Rodrigode Padron   Where policemen eat.
O Remanso Dos Patos   Tel. 988.200.304
                                   www.ORemansoDosPatos.es

FRANCE

ANGOULÊME

Office de Tourisme   2 place Saint Pierre, 16000
                                   Angoulême, France, Tel. 45.95.16.84
Grand Hotel de France   1 place Halles. Tel. 95.47.95
Restaurant La Chamade   13 rampe d'Aguesseau

ANNECY

Hotels and Restaurants

Auberge de l'Eridan   7 avenue de Chavoires, Petit Port,
                                   74000 Annecy le Vieux
                                   Tel. 50.60.22.04
Auberge de Père Bise   74290 Veyrier du Lac, Tailloires
                                   Tel. 50.60.72.01
Hôtel de l'Abbaye   74290 Veyrier du Lac, Tailloires
                                   Tel. 50.67.40.88
Carlton   5 rue Glières, 74000 Annecy
                                   Tel. 50.45.47.75
Le Fréti   12 rue Sainte-Claire, 74000 Annecy
                                   Tel. 50.51.29.52
Splendid   4 quai E-Chappuis, 74000 Annecy
                                   Tel. 50.45.20.00

194

Super-Panorama	Route du Semnoz, 74000 Annecy Tel. 50.45.34.86
Tresoms et de la Forét	3 boulevard de la Corniche, 74000 Annecy Tel. 50.51.43.84

COGNAC

Royal Cognac Barge Tour	Quiz Tour, Mlle. Colette Tassel, 19 rue d'Athenes, 75009 Paris, France. Tel. 48.74.75.30.31
Cognac Brandy Tour	Chez Richon. Segonzac, France. Tel. 45.83.43.05
St. Jacque Gate	quai Papin on Charente River (Only two towers left).
Rue Salnier	Port where sea salt was exported.
Rue du Palais	Law Court and Hôtel de Ville
Church of St. Leger	Named for seventh-century bishop of Autun. Enemies blinded him, cut off his lips, and pulled his tongue out. Imprisoned and executed 656 A.D.
Musée de Cognac	Collection of Emile Gallé's glassware.
Ole Houses	On rue Grande.
Place des Armes	An old stage post and office.
Théâtre Chai de la Comédie	rue des Cordeliers (ex-monastery).

Hotels and Restaurants

Hôtel François	3 place, François. Tel. 45.32.07.18
Mapotel Le Valois	34 rue du 14, Juillet. Tel. 45.82.19.53

Le Logis de Beaulieu   St. Laurant de Cognac.
                                    Tel. 45.82.30.50
Le Coq d Or   33 place, François. Tel. 45.82.07.51
Les Pigeons Blancs   10 rue, Jules-Brisson.
                                    Tel. 45.82.16.36

COLOMBEY LES DEUX ÉGLISES

Hotel   Les Dhuits R.N. 52330.
                                    Tel. 25.01.50.01

GRENOBLE

Office de Tourisme   14 rue de la Republique

Hotels and Restaurants

Park Hotel   10 place Paul, Mistral.
                                    Tel: 76.87.29.11
Angleterre   5 place Victor Hugo.
                                    Tel: 76.87.37.21
Ibis I   Lot des Trois, Dauphin's.
                                    Tel: 76.47.48.49
Chez la Mer Ticket   13 rue Jean Jacques Rousseau.
                                    Tel. 76.44.40
La Jarden de Ville   quai Stephane Jay Quai.
                                    Tel. 76.42.400.06

HONFLEUR

Satie Museum	9 rue Haute. Home of Eric Satie, artist and composer. A fun museum that includes his imaginative art work and early Scott Joplin music.
Saint Catherine of Alexandria's Church	15th-century all-wood church. Made by ship builders with axes. Roof resembles upside down bottom of a ship.
St. Stephen's Church	Now a folklore museum.
Ferne St. Simon Inn	Above the Seine where the Impressionists met.

Statues and Memorials of Samuel de Champlain

Canada	Montreal, Quebec City, New Brunswick, Ontario, Nova Scotia
United States	Lake Champlain (Straddles the border between northern New York State and Vermont. Extends slightly across the border into Canada.) Vermont—Burlington, Isle La Motte New York—Crown Point, Ticonderoga
France	Honfleur, Brouage, Paris

JARNAC

Restaurant	de Château Route 141 La Ribaudiere in Bourg

NICE

Musée Massena	History of Nice and works of Roal Dufy.
Hotel Negresco	37 promenade des Anglais
Garibaldi Square	Statue of Giuseppi Garibaldi.
Quai des États Unis	Where huts of ancient Greeks once stood.
Castle Rock Hill	Top of hill at the end of quai des États Unis, where the dukes of Savoy once had a castle, and where huts of ancient Greeks once stood. Today, a terraced garden with a spectacular view of the city.
Chapel of Black Penitents	Known as Misericordes (goodness).
Church of St. Martin	Where Garibaldi was baptized July 10, 1807.

EVENTS

Carnival	February 13–25th
Jazz Festival	July 21–28th
Musicalia	August (Wednesdays and Saturdays)
Battle of Flowers	Thursday after Ash Wednesday

PARIS

Lido de Paris	116 bis Champs Élysees, 75008 Paris. Tel. 011-33.14561.19.41, Métro George V
Office of Tourisme	6 place Aristide Briand. Tel. 03.23.96.55

Tour Guide and Interpréter	Rosiana Venezian, 74 boulevard du Dr. A. Netter, 75012, Paris. Tel. 1/43.41.01.60, Fax: 1/43.41.01.55, Cell: 06.81.21.41.97, email rosiana@noos.fr
Le Grand Véfour	17 rue de Beaujolais. Tel. 01.42.96.56.27
Maxim's	3 rue Royale. Founded 1893. During the 1970s it was the most expensive restaurant in the world. Present owner Pierre Cardin, fashion designer.
Cardin's Art Nouveau Museum	Above restaurant. Guided tours afternoons except Monday and Tuesday.
Jules Verne	Restaurant in Eiffel Tower. Tel. 01.45.55.61.44
Café Marly	Inside the Louvre.
Canal St. Martin	Reservations: Quiz-Paris Canal 19 rue d'Athénes, 7500 Paris 2:30 p.m. from Bassin de la vilette N.E. Paris Take Métro Jean Jaures Stope.
Crusée Carnavalet	23 rue de Sevigné. Tel. 01.44.59.58.58

PARIS CEMETERIES
Where Famous People Are Buried

La Chapelle Expiatoire	Philippe Égalité, (duc d'Orléans), Charlotte Corday
Montmartre	Degas, Alexandre Dumas (*fils*), Gautier, Berlioz

Montparnasse	Maupassant, Saint Saëns, Brancusi
Pantheon	Voltaire, Victor Hugo, Berthelot, Louis Braille, Jean Moulin, etc.
Passy (near Eiffel Tower)	Manet, Debussy, Berthe Morisat, Fauré
Père Lachaise	Edith Piaf, Chopin, Molière, La Fontaine, de Lesseps, Champollion, Doré, Lalique, Daumier, Corot, Daudet, Sarah Bernhardt, Rachel, Pissarro, Beaumarchais, Balzac, Surat, Bizet, Enesco, Isadora Duncan, Haussmann, Abelard and Héloise
Sainte Catherine	Mirabeau
Saint Étienne du Mont	Racine, Pasçal, Marat, Sainte Geneviève
Saint Germaine des Prés	Descartes
Saint Vincent	Utrillo, Steinlen

PERIGUEUX

St. Front Cathedral	Visit the Cloister. place Bugeaud is the central square.
Monoprix Department Store and Nouvelles Galleries	rue de-la-Republique
Old Quarter	Renaissance houses. Some go back 900 years.
Musée du Perigord	rue Barbecane. Kids will love it, especially the 35-million-year-old skeleton.

Remains of Roman Amphitheatre in the public garden.

Hotels and Restaurants

Domino Hotel	21 place Franceville
Restaurant Le Madelèine	Paté de Perigord

SARLAT

Place de la Liberty	Outdoor cafés.
Bishops Palace	Now a theatre.
Market Square	An outdoor theatre—last week in June through first week in August.
Lantern des Morts	Twelfth-century Tower.
Musée de le Sacred Art	
Place des Oies	Marketplace (Saturdays) In front of Hotel de Ville.
Department Store	Grand Fabrique rue de la Republique
B. Pauliac Bakery	A great place to pick up some rye bread.
La Madelèine Hotel	place de la Petite Rigaudie, Tel. 53.59.12.40

TROYES

Hotels and Restaurants

Hotel Le Champ des Oiseaux	near the Cathedral 20 rue Linard Gonthier. Fax. 03.25.80.98.34
Hotel Le Relais Saint Jean	Underground parking. 51 rue Paillot de Montabert

Au Jardin Gourmand	31 rue Paillot de Montabert
Buy	Prunelle de Troyes brandy
Cellier Saint Pierre	1 place Saint Pierre
Factory Outlet Centres	McArthur Glen Mall, Marques Avenue, Marques City (open air mall). Five-minute bus ride from train station. Special sales January and July. Closed Monday morning and Sunday.

VILLERS COTTÉRETS

Alexandre Dumas Museum	24 rue Demoustler, Birthplace of Alexandre Dumas, Père
Hotel de Ville	Where Dumas' Père's parents married.
Office of Tourisme	6 place Aristid Briand, Tel. 03.23.96.55.10

Nazi Atrocities in Southwestern France

Tulle	Near Limoges, hundreds deported to concentration camps. Ninety-nine returned.
Malle	In Perigord region near Limoges, 120 hostages shot.
Paleul	Near Sarlat, twenty-eight women burned with gasoline.
Rodez	Mid Pyrenees, twenty-three hostages shot.

Oradoure Sur Glane	642 men, women, children burned to death.
Mende	Entire population shot.
Sarlat	Civilians impaled on hooks in butcher shops.

Museums and Memorials to Giuseppe Garibaldi

United States	Meucci—Garibaldi Museum; House of Antonio Meucci, where Garibaldi stayed; Richmond Borough, Tompkins Avenue, Staten Island, NY. Monuments in Washington Park, Greenwich Village, New York City.
Sicily	Calatafimi, Palermo, Milazzo, Messina
Italy	Naples, Rome (Janiculum Hill), Venice, Lake Como
Brazil	Buenos Aires

BIBLIOGRAPHY

BASQUE COUNTRY

Brodrick, James. *Saint Ignatuis Loyola, The Pilgrim Years*. New York: Farrar, Straus & Cudahy, 1958.

Clark, Robert P. *Beyond The Basque French Years and Beyond*. Reno, NV: University of Nevada Press, 1979.

Eye Witness Travel. *Northern Spain*. Hudson, NY: D.K. Publishing, Inc., 2007.

Gautier, Theophile. *A Romantic Spain*. New York: Alfred A. Knopf, 1926.

Gordan, Thomas S. and Max Morgan Witts. *Guernica, the Crucible of WW II*. New York: Stein and Day, 1975.

Gordan, Thomas S. *Guernica and Total War*. New York: Stein and Day, 1975.

Kurlansky, Mark. *The Basque History of the World*. New York: Walker Publishing Co., 1999.

Laxalt, Robert. *In a Hundred Graves; A Basque Portrait*. Reno, NV: University of Nevada Press, 1972.

Lowney, Chris. *A Vanished World.* New York: Oxford University Press, 2006.

Masnik, Yasna. *The Basque Country (Vacances).* Paris: Hachette Publisher, 2002.

Maynard, Theodore. *Ignatius and The Jesuits.* New York: P.J. Kennedy & Sons, 1957.

Montguerre, Jean Marc. *St. Francis Xavier.* Garden City, NY: Doubleday & Co., 1963.

Patterson, Ian. *Guernica.* Cambridge, MA: Harvard University Press, 2007.

Slocombe, George. *William the Conquer Changed the History of England.* New York: G.P. Putnam's Sons, 1961.

Starkie, Walter F. *Road to Santiago.* New York: E.P. Dutton & Co., Inc., 1958.

Stokstad, Marilyn. *Santiago de Compostela.* Norman, OK: University of Oklahoma Press, 1978.

Symington, Andy. *Northern Spain.* New York: Footprint Books, Sterling Publishing Co., 2000.

Thomas, Gordon and Max Morgan Witts. *Guernica.* New York: Stein and Day, 1991.

FRANCE

Anderson, Erica. *The World of Albert Schweitzer.* New York: Harper Brothers, 1955.

Ardagh, John. *The Book of France.* Secaucus, NY: Chartwell Books, Inc., 1980.

Aubrac, Raymond. *The French Resistance.* Paris: Hagen Editions,1997.

Belloc, Hilaire. *Richelieu Study*. Philadelphia: J.B. Lippincott Publisher, 1929.

Berlioz, Hector. *Hector Berlioz Memoirs*. New York: Harcourt Brace, 1966.

Blanch, Lesley. *Pierre Loti—The Legendary Romantic*. New York: Harcourt Brace, Jovanovich, 1982.

Blanch, Lesley. *Pierre Loti*. New York: Harcourt Brace, Jovanovich, 1983.

Bordeaux, Henry. *St. Francis de Sales, The Theologian of Love*. London: Longmans, Green and Co., 1929.

Brazon, James. *Albert Schweitzer*. New York: G.P. Putnam's Sons, 1975.

Brown, Karen. *Karen Brown's France*. New York: Fodor's Travel Publications, 2002.

Brody, Elaine. *Paris: The Musical Kaleidoscope 1870–1925*. New York: George Braziller, 1987.

Brower, Harriet. *Story Lives of Master Musicians*. Freeport, NY: Books for Libraries Press, 1971.

Brown, T. Graham and Sir Gavin de Beer. *The First Ascent of Mont Blanc*. London: Oxford University Press, 1957.

Cartellieri, Otto. *Court of Burgundy*. New York: Haskell House Publishers, 1970.

Champagne, Ardennes. *France*. Leconte, France: Estel Blois Productions, 1997.

Charvet, P.E. *Literary History of France, Vol. IV*. London: Ernest Benn Ltd., 1967.

Cubertson, Judi and Tom Randall, *Permanent Parisians*. New York: Walker, 1996.

D'Orliac, Jehanne. *Francis I, Prince of the Renaissance*. Philadelphia: J. B. Lippincot, 1932.

de Gaulle, Charles. *The Complete War Memories of Charles de Gaulle.* New York: de Capo Press, 1984.

de Rouvroy, Louis, duc de Saint-Simon. *Historical Memoirs of Duc de Saint Simon, Vol. I.* New York: McGraw Hill, 1969.

Dumas, Alexandre. *Black Tulip.* New York: P.F. Collier and Son, 1948.

Dumas, Alexandre. *On Board the Emma.* New York: D. Appleton Co., 1929.

Elliot, J.H. *Berlioz,The Master Musicians.* New York: Farrar, Straus & Giradoux, 1967.

Elliot, J.H. *Berlioz.* New York: Farrar, Straus, & Giradoux, 1967.

Emanuel, Frank. *The New World of Henri Saint Simon.* Cambridge, MA: Harvard University Press, 1956.

Endore, Guy. *King of Paris.* New York: Simon & Schuster, 1956.

European Travel Commission. *Visit Europe.* New York: Einar Gustavson, 1956.

Fernandenz, Dominique. *Romanian Rhapsody: An Overlooked Corner of Europe.* New York: Algora, 2000.

Gaffney, Patrick. *St. Louis de-Montfort.* Bayshore, NY: Montfort, 1976.

Galante, Pierre. *The General.* New York: Random House, 1968.

Geraghty, Tony. *March or Die (French Foreign Legion).* New York: Facts on File, 1986.

Gillmor, Alan M. *Erik Satie (Twaynes' Music Series).* New York: Macmillan, 1988.

Golinsky, Francoise Marie and Alice Vidal. *The Love of France.* London: Octopus Books, 1977.

Hackitt, David. *Champlain's Dream.* New York: Simon & Schuster, 2008.

Haloman, Kern D. *Berlioz*. Cambridge, MA: Harvard University Press, 1989.

Haloman, Kern D. *Bartholdi*. Cambridge, MA: Riverside Press, 1964.

Hardwick, Mollie. *Lady Hamilton*. New York: Holt Rinehart & Winston, 1969.

Hatch, Alden. *The de Gaulle Nobody Knows*. New York: Hawthorne Books, 1960.

Hemmings, F.W. *Alexandre Dumas, King of Romance*. New York: Scribner, 1980.

Herald, Christopher. *André Malraux*. New York: Harmony Books,1980.

Horne, Sir Alistair. *The Terrible Year*. New York: Viking Press, 1972.

Horne, Sir Alistair. *The Serge of Paris and The Commune*. New York: Penguin, 1979.

Huddleston, Sisley. *France, the Tragic Years*. New York: Devin Adair, 1955.

Johnson, Diane. *Into a Paris Quarter*. Washington, DC: National Geographic, 2005.

Kane, Robert. *France at its Best*. Lincolnwood, IL: Passport Books, 1986.

Lacouture, Jean. *André Malraux*. New York: Pantheon, 1977.

Ladurie, Emanuel. *Times of Feasts and Times of Famine*. Garden City, NY: Doubleday, 1971.

Lombard, Charles M. *Xavier de Maistre*. Boston: Twayne, 1977.

Lombard, Charles M. *Joseph de Maistre*. Boston: Twayne, 1976.

Loomis, Stanley. *Paris in the Terror*. New York: Richardson & Steirman, 1964.

Lord, John. *Beacon Lights of History*. Syracuse, NY: Ford, Howard and Hurlburt, 1884.

Loti, Pierre. *Pierre Loti, Notes of My Youth.* New York: Doubleday, Page & Co., 1924.

Loti, Pierre. *An Iceland Fisherman.* New York: Alfred A. Knopf, 1946.

Manceron, Claude. *Their Gracious Pleasure.* New York: Alfred A. Knopf, 1980.

Messner, Julian. J. *Alvin Kugelmass.* New York: Simon & Schuster, 1972.

Oberthur, Mariel. *Cafés & Cabarets of Montmartre.* Salt Lake City: Peregrine Smith Books, 1984.

Parkman, Francis. *Pioneers of France in the New World.* Williamstown, MA: Corner House Publishers, 1970.

Pastene, Jerome. *Three Quarter Time.* New York: Abelard Press, 1951.

Picht, Werner. *Albert Schweitzer.* New York: Harper Row, 1964.

Ross, Michael. *Alexandre Dumas.* Newton Abbot: David & Charles, 1981.

Rostand, Edmond. *Chanticleer.* New York: Macmillan, 1921.

Russell, Jack. *Nelson and the Hamiltons.* New York: Simon & Schuster, 1969.

Russell, John. *Paris.* New York: Harry N. Abrams, 1983.

Sanders, E.K. *Fénélon.* London: Green & Co., 1901.

Satie, Erik. *The Collective Writings of Erik Satie.* London: Atlas Press, 1996.

Satie, Erik. *Parade.* Mineola, NY: Dover, 2000.

Satie, Erik. *The Writings of Erik Satie.* London: Eulenbarg, 1980.

Saunders, Edith. *Age of Worth.* Bloomington, IN: Indiana University Press, 1955.

Savage, Katherine. *The Story of the Second World War*. Paris: Oxford University Press, 1967.

Schoenbrun, David. *Soldiers of the Night*. New York: E.P. Dutton, 1980.

Schoops, Claude. *Alexandre Dumas, Genius of Life*. New York: Franklin Watts, 1988.

Schweitzer, Albert. *Letters*. New York: Macmillan, 1992.

Scola, Paul. *Alps and Jura*. New Jersey: Hunter Publishing, 1995.

Scott, Janet Mary. *St. Jane de Chantal*. London: Sands, 1948.

Sikes, Ralph and Paula Harper. *Pissarro, His Life and Works*. New York: Horizon Press, 2004.

Simms, Annabel. *An Hour from Paris*. London: Pallas Athene Ltd., 2002.

Stakes, Frederick A. *Pierre, Loti, "A Tale of the Pyreness 'Romuntcho'"*. New York: Stakes, 1923.

Stein, Rose Ellen. *Pierre Loti*. New York: Doubleday, Page & Co., 1924.

Sulzberger, C.L. *The Last of the Giants*. New York: Macmillan, 1970.

Tapie, Victor. *France in the Age of Louis' XIII and Richelieu*. New York: Macmillan, 1974.

Todd, Oliver. <u>*André Malraux, A Life.*</u> New York: Alfred A. Knopf, 2005.

Trotta, Liz. *Jude*. New York: Harper Collins, 1998.

Tucker, Alan, ed. *Penguin Guide to France*. New York: Penguin Books, 1991.

Volta, Ornella. *Satie Seen Through His Letters*. London: Marion Boyars, 2000.

Wade, Richard. *Companion Guide to the Loire*. Englewood Cliffs: Prentice Hall, 1983.

Werner, Laurie T. *Pierre Loti, Island Fisherman*. London: Laurie Werner, Ltd., London & Frederick Stakes Co., 1924.

Wertenbaker, Lael. *The World of Picasso, Visionary*. New York: Time Life Books, 1969.

Whitelaw, Nancy. *Charles de Gaulle: "I Am France"*. New York: Dillon Press, 1991.

Wilkens, Burke. *Francis In All His Glory*. New York: Farrar Straus, Giradoux, 1972.

Williams, Charles. *The Last Great Frenchman*. New York: J. Wiley & Sons, 1997.

SICILY

Astarita, Tommaso. *Between Salt Water and Holy Water*. New York: W.W. Norton & Co., 2005.

Belford, Ros. *The Rough Guide to Italy*. London: Rough Guides, 2003.

Bernhardt, August. *How the Pope Became Infallible*. Garden City, NY: Doubleday, 1981.

Birmingham, Brenda, ed. *Eyewitness Travel Guide, Naples and the Amalfi Coast*. New York: 2003.

Burton, Jean. *Garibaldi, Knight of Liberty*. New York: Alfred A. Knopf, 1945.

Butler, Michael. *Fodor's City Pack Naples 25 Best*. New York: Fodor's Travel Publications, 2005.

Croce, Benedetto. *History of Kingdom of Naples*. Chicago: University of Chicago Press, 1970.

Dumas, Alexander. *On Board the Emma*. New York; Appleton & Co., 1929.

Bibliography

Este, Carlo D'. *Bitter Victory* and *The Battle for Sicily. New York:* E.P. Dutton, 1988.

Eye Witness Travel Guides. *Sicily*. New York: D.K. Publishing, 2003.

Fodor's Naples, Capri and the Amalfi Coast, Fodor's Travel Publications, 2004.

Garwood, Duncan. "Naples and the Amalfi Coast." *The Lonely Planet* (2005). http://www.lonelyplanet.com/italy/campania/naples-the-amalfi-coast.

Hibbert, Christopher. *Garibaldi and His Enemies*. New York: New American Library, 1966.

Honnor, Juluis. *Footprint*. Naples, Italy, 2005.

Insight Guide to Southern Italy. London: APA Publications, 2002.

Kennedy, Jeffrey. *Eyewitness Naples and Amalfi Coast*. London: Dorling Kindersley Ltd., 2004.

Lewis, Norman. *In Sicily*. New York: St. Martin's Press, 2002.

Lindquist, Willis. *Universal History of The World Christianity and Byzantine Vol. IV*. New York: Golden Press, 1966.

MacSmith, Denis. *Cavour*. New York: Alfred A. Knopf, 1985.

MacSmith, Denis. *History of Sicily*. New York: Viking Press, 1987.

Melena, Elpis. *Garibaldi's Memoirs*. Sarasota, FL: International Institute of Garibaldi Studies, 1981.

Naples and the Amalfi Coast, Bath, UK: 2005.

Price, Willadene. *Bartholdi and the Statue of Liberty*. Chicago: Rand McNally, 1959.

Rhodes, Anthony. *The Vatican in The Age of Dictators*. New York: Harcourt, Brace, 1973.

Rhodes, Anthony. *Vatican in Age of Dictators*. New York: Holt, Rinehardt, Winston, 1973.

Ridley, Jasper. *Garibaldi Constable*. London: 1974.

Ridley, Jasper. *Garibaldi*. New York: Viking Press, 1976.

Rioll, Lucy. *Garibaldi, Lion of Caprera*. New Haven: Yale University Press, 2007.

Sheen, Bishop Fulton. *The World's First Love*. San Francisco: Ignatuis Press, 1996.

Siaky, A.A. *Farewell to Salonica*. New York: Wyn Publishing, 1946.

Travel Guides. *Sicily*. Greenville, SC: Michelin Travel Publication, 1998.

Sicily in Your Pocket. Greenville, SC: Michelin Travel Publication, 1998.

Sicily Eyewitness Travel Guides. London: DK Publishing, 2003.

World's Great Speeches. New York: Dover, 1970.

Tullio, Paolo. *North of Naples, South of Rome*. New York: St. Martin's Press, 1999.

Viola, Herman J. and Susan P. *Giuseppe Garibaldi*. New Haven: Chelsea House Publishers, 1988.

MORE THANKS

BASQUE COUNTRY

SANTIAGO, SPAIN
Arturo Lopez Quintela, Professor
University of Santiago de Compostela

PARIS and SUBURBS

Christian David "Le Grand Véfour"
M. Bernard Etienne "The Lido"
Georgia Geerling
Jim Haynes
Sandrine and Aubert Scagnetto
Rosiana and Jean Guy Venezian

MONTROUGE
Marie and Michel Popov

SURESNES
Gabrielle Mihaescu

BOUGIVAL
Sandrine and Christophe Verrier

FOURQUEUX
Rita and Philippe Lecat

ST. GERMAIN EN LAYE
Anne Marie and Francis Detourbet

FRANCE

GUICHEN
Jacqueline and Gaston Scagnetto

ST. HELEN
Christiane and Alexis Etienne

BRUERA ALLI CHAMPS
Rosanne and Robert Strouts

VALENCE
Guy I Sanjan
Conseil Général de la Drôme

CLERMONT FERRAND
Danielle and Georges Lebard

VILLENEUVE SUR LOT
Celine Leygues Raphel

NOLAY
Jill and Pascal Labranche

DIJON
Micheline Laby

AINAY LE VIEIL
Marie France de Peyronnet

STRASBOURG
Francis Carpentier
Julie and Robert Carpentier
Paulette Amrheim

LUNAY
Corinne and Serge Aubert

ANNECY
Sister Marie Therese Bricard (Monastery de la Visitation)

ORANGE
Mireille Finnegan (Hotel Lou Cigaloun)

NÎMES
Sylvianne and Francis Mercier

MAZU
Marie France Sokolowski

ENTZHEIM
Anne Marie Pham

AVIGNON
Pierre Teocchi

UNITED STATES

DALLAS, TEXAS
Isabelle de Wulf, former Executive Director
French American Chamber of Commerce

COLD SPRINGS, TEXAS
Ladelle Zielinsky

CONTACTS

TOUR GUIDE AND INTERPRÉTER
Rosiana Venezian
74 Boulevard du Dr. A. Netter, 75012, Paris
Tel: 1/43.41.01.60,
Fax: 1/43.41.01.55,
email: rosiana@noos.fr,
Cell: 06.81.21.41.97

ROYAL COGNAC BARGE TOUR
Quiz Tour, Mlle. Colette Tassel, 19 rue d'Athenes,
75009 Paris, France Tel. 48.74.75.30.31

COGNAC BRANDY TOUR
Chez Richon
16130 Segonzac, France
Tel. 45.83.43.05

RAIL EUROPE
(808) 438-7245

NATIONAL MUSEUM OF FRANCE-AMERICAN COOPERATION
33 place du Général Leclerc
Blérancourt, France
www.blerancourt.com

QUIZ-PARIS CANAL
19 rue d'Athènes
2:30 p.m. From Bassin de la Vilette N.E. Paris
Take Métro Jean Jaures Stop

TIMELINE

GIUSEPPE GARIBALDI

1836 South America

1848—Leaves South America. Back to Italy 1848.
Rejected by King Charles Albert.
King's troops defeated.
Austrians return.
Milanese murdered.
Escapes to fight his own war. 1849—1st war in Lombardy.

1849 Return to Nice

First war against Papal States.
Republic lasts one month.
Austrians defeat King Charles Albert, who resigns.
Garibaldi defeats Papal troops and French army.
Reinforcements at Rome vs. Garibaldi.
Anita arrives.
Retreat.
Pursued by four armies.
Safe arrival in Piedmont, the one state in Italy with a constitution.
Arrested in Genoa. Released.
Ordered to leave Italy.
1850-1853—One-day visit in Nice, then Tangiers and New York City.

1854 England

Return to Nice.
Visits by Emma Roberts, Jessie White and Baroness von Schwartz.
Buys Caprera (half of it).
1856—Ordered to Turin by King Victor Emmanuel.
Told of Double Diplomacy and France's agreement to help fight Austrians.
Victor Emmanuel needs him to fight Austrians.
Made a General in Piedmontese army.
Sent to mountains in Lombardy for second time.
1859—Napoleon III makes secret treaty with Austrian Emperor Franz-Joseph.
Garibaldi learns Nice has been given to France.

1860 Sicily

Arrives in Marsala.
First Battle at Calatafimi (Miracle of the Stones).

Palermo

Top of three mountains. Led men in circles. Attacked enemy from behind.
Surrender of Palermo.
Alexandre Dumas arrives. Occupies Royal Palace.

Milazzo (Cape of Milazzo)

Sneaked ships around to opposite side of fort. Attacked fort from behind.

Messina

Where do I sign?
Strait of Messina.
Volunteers on sand at Faro Point. Kept enemy focused on Faro while he took first force across the strait.
Across strait to Reggio in southern Italy.
S.O.S. to Naples for permission to surrender.

Mop-Up Operations

Garibaldi goes on ahead to Salerno.
Dumas arrives in Salerno.
King Francis flies to Gaeta.
Dumas provides fireworks.
Garibaldi on train to Naples.
Naples wild welcome.
Corrupt government (two months).
Army billeted outside Naples at Caserta.
Garibaldi occupies Royal Palace.
Battle of Volturno against Neapolitans.
Garibaldi defeats King Francis II; more miracles, fog and enemy that disobeyed orders.
King Victor Emmanuel defeats Papal Troops.
King takes possession of Neapolitan province.
Garibaldi and Thousand dismissed. No longer needed.
1860—Back to Caprera.
Agrees not to invade Tyrol.
1861, 1862—Back to Sicily.
Battle at Aspromonte.
Can't fight fellow Italians. Wounded in foot below ankle.
Imprisoned.
Back to Caprera.
1864—England.
Sons and friends ignored. English friends buy rest of Caprera.
1866—Lombardy 3rd Time.
Ordered to Retreat (Venice becomes part of Italy).
Visit to Venice. Calls for march on Rome.
1867—March on Rome 2nd Time.
Arrested before dawn at Orvieto. Back to Caprera.
Escape with dyed hair.
Pops up in Florence.
1870, 1871—Off to France. Only General to win a battle.
Shouted down in French Assembly.
Escape from Prussians.
1870, 1871—Victor Emmanuel takes Rome.
Popes prefer to be prisoners in Vatican for sixty years.
1882—Dies age 74, on June 2.
Picture of mother on wall.

Other Books by Mary Jane Wilson

EUROPE with a BUSY BODY (1985)
BACK to EUROPE with the BUSY BODY (2006)

To Order, Visit:

www.waldobrucepublishing.com
Email: waldobrucepublishing@yahoo.com

Made in the USA
San Bernardino, CA
27 May 2017